AF539265

THE HOLIDAY YARDS OF FLORENCIO MORALES

"EL HOMBRE DE LAS BANDERAS"

Amy V. Kitchener

University Press of Mississippi   Jackson

Dedicated to the Morales family of Los Angeles and Teoloyucan

Photo Credits: Amy Kitchener, front cover; Mary MacGregor-Villarreal, plate 24; unknown photographer, photos courtesy Morales Martínez family of Teoloyucan, pp. 8 and 30 and plates 30, 32, 35, 36 and 39; all other photos by the author.

97 96 95 94 4 3 2 1

Library of Congress Cataloging-in-Publication Data

Kitchener, Amy V.
The holiday yards of Florencio Morales, "el Hombre de las Banderas" / by Amy V. Kitchener.
p. cm. — (Folk art and artists series)
Includes bibliographical references.

ISBN: 978-1-61703-332-2

1. Morales, Florencio, 1949-1992—Criticism and interpretation. 2. Outsider art—California—Los Angeles. 3. Assemblage (Art)—California—Los Angeles. 4. Garden ornaments and furniture—California—Los Angeles. I. Morales, Florencio, 1949-1992. II. Title. III. Series.
N6537.M642K58 1994
709'.2—dc20 93-48421
CIP

British Cataloging-in-Publication data available

CONTENTS

Preface 5

Florencio Morales:
"El Hombre de las Banderas" 7

Halloween 10

Christmas 19

Other Holidays 24

Influences, Aesthetics, and Style 29

Aftermath 33

References 35

Color Plates 37

PREFACE

I first learned of Florencio Morales's holiday art in October 1989. A short article titled "Gardener Raises Bumper Crop of Ghouls," which appeared in the *Los Angeles Times,* piqued my interest. Motivated by a long fascination with "yard art" and domestic yards, I went to see Morales's construction and gazed in amazement at a scene both gory and satirical. As I stood at the fence, examining the individual items, many passersby stopped and did the same. The children especially loved it, simultaneously showing fear and enchantment.

During this visit I met Florencio, who invited me inside the yard for a closer look. He excitedly explained the nature of his characters' exploits. A witch in a tree hungered for baby's blood, but since she couldn't find any, she settled for a chicken's. Another figure was killed by the devil when she went to a dance hall unescorted, against her parents' orders. Dozens of other strange creatures inhabited Florencio's yard, each one conveying a message. Intrigued by Florencio and his art, I asked if I could document his display as the basis of a university course paper. Florencio enthusiastically agreed. I photographed his yard and tape recorded interviews with him and his neighbors, desiring to understand his motivations and to learn about his artistic process and about the effects his assemblages had on him and the community.

During the next three years, from 1989 to 1992, Florencio and I visited on many occasions. I had completed my paper and he was no longer an "informant" but a friend. Sometimes I came by just to chat, other times to see his exhibits on holidays such as Christmas and Valentine's Day. I found these times inspiring. As a newcomer to Los Angeles in 1989, I felt unconnected to any community. From the outside, looking in, the city seemed like a series of unrelated faces, buildings and freeway exchanges. Through his displays and celebrations, Florencio expressed warmth and generosity, creating a forum in which many others and I could interact and enjoy each other. In his yard we felt we belonged.

A year after meeting Florencio, during the Halloween season of 1990, I learned he was terminally ill. Although debilitated, he continued assembling his holiday yards until his death in October 1992. In April 1993, I unearthed my original research and interviewed more of his family members and friends in order to gain greater insight into the man and his art. This book is the result.

I am greatly indebted to Florencio Morales and to his family, friends and neighbors for providing both the inspiration and the materials for this book. His brothers, Alberto Morales Martínez and Alfonso Morales Martínez, and his sister-in-law, Carolina Ramírez Morales, enriched my understanding of Florencio's life and art. Cristina Díaz, a neighbor, offered astute observations about the Halloween assemblage as did Paul Jenkins, another resident of Griffin Avenue. Peter Quezada generously shared his experience with Florencio, including describing the process of creating the mural he painted to honor him. I would also like to thank Petri Gonzáles, who was a boarder in the Moraleses' house, for her kindness and sharing of information, and Ed Boyer, a reporter at the *Los Angeles Times,* for tracking down file photos and offering me the names of his contacts.

I immensely appreciate the technical assistance of Alex Todorovic, who provided simultaneous translations in English and Spanish during an interview with Alberto, Alfonso, and Carolina Morales and then went on to transcribe and translate the tapes and offer his perspective. I am grateful to Karen Seger for her critical reading of the original manuscript. Thanks to David Grand for his moral and editorial support, and for making his famous lasagna so that I could take it to one of the Morales family interviews. Finally, I am indebted to Michael Owen Jones, whose idea it was to bring my research to publication in this series, and whose constant encouragement and tireless editorial expertise made this book a reality.

Florencio Morales: "El Hombre de las Banderas"

Mexican American, Gardener, and Artist

On Halloween night in 1990, the street was jammed with cars passing slowly by a house on Griffin Avenue in Los Angeles (plate 1). Amidst the hundreds of people in costume gathered on the sidewalk, vendors sold tacos, corn on the cob and popsicles. The air was filled with loud moans and the screams of demons and spooks emanating from a speaker hidden in a tree. Spotlights and torches shed light on bloodied and disfigured corpses left partially unburied in shallow graves full of writhing body parts. Meanwhile, a mummy struggled to break out of a coffin (plate 2), a skeleton posed with his scythe (plate 3), and a legless witch stalked her prey from a tree covered in cobwebs and copper kitchen utensils (plate 4). Looming above, a blood-red devil clad in a dinner jacket and Wellington boots beckoned the multitude below to come closer (plate 5). An entourage of wigged ghosts accompanied him (plate 6). Grotesque drunkards lay in a heap on the ground, one of them proclaiming, *"Beber es un placer, sigue mi consejo—ja ja ja ja ja"* ("Drinking is a pleasure, follow my advice—ha ha ha ha ha"). An eerie mist generated by a fog machine enveloped everything, including the onlookers.

Florencio Morales, the creator of this spectacular scene, was known throughout Los Angeles for his elaborate and original holiday yard displays. He received a great deal of publicity from the local news broadcasts and various newspapers that featured his exhibits over the years. In the northeast section of the city where he lived, many people referred to him simply as *"El Hombre de las Banderas"* ("the Man of the Flags") because he often included flags as a prominent motif in his displays, and he always flew American, Mexican, and California flags over his home. From 1981 until 1992, Florencio created scenes to commemorate various Mexican, American, and Mexican American holidays—Halloween, Thanksgiving, Christmas, St. Valentine's Day, Easter, Mother's Day, *Cinco de Mayo,* Memorial Day, Fourth of July, August 13 (the anniversary of the Treaty of Teoloyucan), and September 16 (Mexican Independence Day). These exhibits served as settings for extravagant and spirited celebrations involving the local community.

The fifth of eight children, Florencio was born in 1949 in Teoloyucan, located in central Mexico approximately forty-five kilometers north of Mexico City. After graduating from high school he worked in a battery factory while pursuing a college degree. Long hours of labor coupled with the demands of academe took its toll on his health. A doctor advised, "If you want to study, study . . . if you want to work, work. But you're doing too much now." Since Florencio had to support himself, he chose work. His brother Alfonso characterized Florencio as a tireless laborer. "He had a lot of stamina when he worked. He was very tough. He liked to work. He always took the hardest and heaviest kinds of work, and he never said that he didn't want to do it. One time his appendix ruptured, and since my father was very strict, he sent him to work. Not until he saw Florencio sprawled out on the ground nearly dying did he call the doctor to save him."

His family spoke of Florencio as a strong-willed leader. "When he came [to the United States] his mother missed him very much because he was the one son who always stood up and said, 'I want us to do this,' and he defended her," said Carolina Morales, his sister-in-law. "If one of the others got angry with his mother, he calmed them down."

In 1973, at the age of twenty-four, Florencio left Mexico and his family in search of a better life in the United States. His mother's brother, who had immigrated to Los Angeles, told him that opportunities for work abounded and welcomed Florencio to stay with him. Life in L. A., however, proved more difficult than his uncle had described. Florencio variously worked in gardening, construction projects, and a furniture shop. Meanwhile, he found himself having trouble with his uncle who was often drunk.

After two or three years of struggling with his uncle's alcoholism, Florencio sought a way to get out on his own. He met an elderly man who lived alone and needed help taking care of himself. The man offered Florencio room and board in return for work as a care giver. Their relationship of mutual support fostered close bonds, so much so that Florencio described the man as "a second father." With his life more secure, Florencio again worked as a gardener, contracting himself out to private residences as well as city parks.

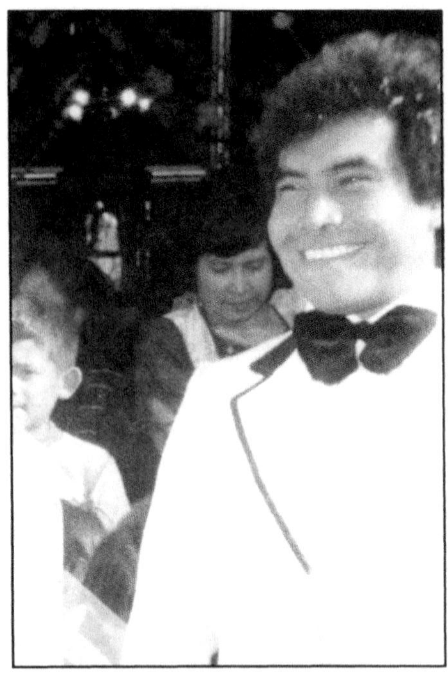
Florencio Morales at his wedding in Teoloyucan, Mexico, 1980.

During these first years in Los Angeles, Florencio maintained strong ties with his family in Teoloyucan, returning every year during the Christmas season. While in Mexico in December 1979, he met his future wife, Alicia, at a party. After communicating long-distance for a year, they became engaged and then married. When Alicia joined Florencio in Los Angeles in 1980, they found an apartment in Montecito Heights, an older residential neighborhood in Lincoln Heights situated in the hills northeast of downtown Los Angeles.

This community, which comprises large numbers of Mexican Americans, Asian Americans and Caucasians, is predominately lower-middle class and middle class. "Mom and Pop" stores dot the street corners. California Craftsman style houses built in the early decades of this century line the streets, and the front yards of homes and apartment buildings are well manicured. Rose bushes grow along chain-link fences, planters on front porches contain varieties of flowers and succulents, and caged birds hang on exterior beams of some homes. People spend time outside, socializing with neighbors, working in their yards, or observing their children at play. Many residents have grown up in this community and stayed to raise their own families. Despite the friendly neighborhood ambience, however, the area has not been immune to the ills of Los Angeles, such as crime, violence, and gang activity.

From this new home base, Florencio pursued work as a free-lance gardener, securing jobs on an informal basis without a "green card." He gradually established himself, acquired more clients, and hired a crew. By 1984, Florencio and Alicia had two children, Atilano and Rosa María, and the family moved to a larger residence on Griffin Avenue. The new house included extra rooms which could be rented out to boarders, a large front yard and a garage in the back of the property.

Florencio created his first display during Halloween in 1981, when he hung a life-size dummy by a noose in the front yard of his rented apartment (similar to plate 7). As Carolina Morales remembered, "That's the only thing he did. He saw that it attracted the attention of people who passed by. Later, when he got his house, he made it bigger. He began putting up trinkets and the tombs." That same year he also assembled a small nativity scene in his front window. He said it gave him the feeling of *la nostalgia* for his family and home in Mexico. The following year he made a larger *nacimiento* (nativity) display, this time placing it in the front yard.

The local response to his holiday assemblages fueled his creativity and provided new ideas for installations. His brother, Alfonso, recalled that "all of the neighbors around here used to say, 'Oh, very beautiful. It's very good.' They would tell him to put [up] more for the next year. And if he didn't have a display for all of the different holidays, like July 4, they would say to him, 'Why don't you put something up for this holiday?' They supported him, gave him ideas. That's why he continued putting it up every year. The people were happy. They were very pleased with what he was doing."

The feeling of satisfaction, his own and the public's, deepened as Florencio modified, refined and elaborated his exhibits. Incorporating new elements for each holiday became Florencio's passion. As a gardener, he made regular trips to the dump to dispose of waste foliage, and he would often return bearing odd items with which to refurbish or augment an upcoming exhibit. He frequented yard sales and secondhand stores to find electrical lights, costumes and other objects that caught his fancy. On many occasions, people brought him things they thought he could use. Instead of housing the mowers and other tools of his trade (which he left out in the driveway), the garage behind his home served as the curatorial vault for his raw materials.

Halloween

On Halloween night in 1990 adults and children formed a procession leading toward an altar in the Moraleses' driveway, constructed in observance of the Roman Catholic holy day of All Souls, which falls on November 2 (plates 8 and 9). Florencio's daughter, Rosa María, and his wife, Alicia, impersonating ghouls, handed out an endless supply of candy to all who attended. Many people knelt and prayed in front of the altar. Some left donations to help defray costs of the event.

Florencio held center stage. He presided under the tree in the driveway dressed as Dracula, staying in character the entire evening. Often he stood completely still, as if he were one of the characters in his display, waiting for someone to pass by; then, raising his arms and flapping his cape, he pretended to pursue the person. He delighted in these surprises, as did his victims, who shrieked at his performance. Mothers with babies approached the "count" and had their pictures taken as he feigned sucking blood from their necks (plate 10). Some participants recorded the dramatic action with video cameras. Petri Gonzáles, one of the Moraleses' boarders, said that Florencio was very ill that night, but he would not leave because of his sense of duty to his guests—members of the community, neighbors and strangers.

The Halloween assemblage always required more preparation and expense than any other holiday display. In the construction, Florencio spread hundreds of objects across the entire front yard and driveway, even utilizing the airspace above his house.

The Halloween exhibit continuously evolved, showing a great amount of change and elaboration from one year to the next (compare plates I and II). He began preparations at the end of September, gradually bringing out his props and installing them one by one in the front yard, creating each aspect of the display himself. Some of the figures were department store mannequins dressed in costume for the occasion, while others he made from scratch by stuffing old clothing and masked heads with straw to create a lifelike effect. Particular presentations required the building of props such as coffins. He modified the topography of his yard to create micro-environments in which various scenes could be set. For instance, he would hang a witch from a dead tree that he had planted for this purpose. To create grave mounds he dug, hauled, and dumped hundreds of pounds of dirt. During the month of October, Florencio was continuously occupied readjusting and embellishing the figures.

His brother, Alfonso, described Florencio's process: "We didn't understand what he had in mind until we saw it, then we said, 'It looks great, it's beautiful.' And from there he made it look even better. He thought about moving it more to one side, or flying a flag, or putting up an uglier rag." Besides expending a tremendous amount of time, Florencio invested hefty sums of money in the display; the electric bill totaled three-hundred to four-hundred dollars, the fog machine rental cost one-hundred dollars, and the candy for the party revellers averaged over two-hundred dollars. Since he acquired his raw materials over a number of years, it is difficult to estimate his total investment, but he must have spent thousands of dollars to create the final product. Although most people embraced his creations, some thought it impractical to spend so much money on something so frivolous. Alfonso remembered, "They would say, 'You're crazy. . . you're crazy. Why are you putting that there? You're just spending your money to let people know what you're doing.' 'No,' he said, 'that doesn't matter. It's my money and I want to do it.' "

Since the public bus stopped directly in front of Florencio's house, many people talked with him and viewed his displays on a daily basis. He reveled in explaining the actions of his characters, because each entity in the yard carried personal or cultural meaning for him. When he was working on his assemblage someone might ask him, "Hey, why are you putting that there?" Florencio would respond with a vivid account. A talented creator of visual illusion, he was also an extraordinary storyteller. His face became animated, and sometimes he even jumped up to act out parts of a story. He might, for example, involve his audience by grabbing a listener's wrist to illustrate how a spirit had grabbed him.

Some of his tales included well-known Mexican legends and personal experience narratives, while others resembled exempla that illustrated moral precepts. Most of the pieces in his yard had placards near them explaining in Spanish the nature of the scene. One of the stories concerned a ghoulish couple on the periphery of the yard. A female figure dressed in formal bridal attire covered with blood stood next to her tuxedo-wearing "groom" who sat in a chair (plate 12). Florencio recounted that a mother refused her daughter permission to go to a dance, but the disobedient daughter insisted on attending. She dressed in her best clothes and went out into the night. On the way she encountered a very handsome and well-dressed man riding a beautiful black horse who offered to escort her to the party. There, they danced together, and she became enraptured, falling under his love spell. They decided to marry that night. She noticed too late that he had the feet of a chicken and was turning into a devil. In the end he killed her.

This story not only refers to the gruesome scene staged in Florencio's display, but also to a widely told Mexican legend known as "The Demon Dancer." Cristina Díaz, a neighbor who took interest in Florencio's festive exhibits, told a different story about the devil and his bride. Ms. Díaz, a teacher from Guadalajara, occasionally brought her students to see Florencio's decorated yards. She recognized the bloody newlyweds as characters from a popular tale told about a couple whose wedding night ended in disaster. When the groom discovered that his bride was not a virgin, he became enraged and killed her. Cristina pointed out that her version explained the presence of the woman's undergarment, which lay symbolically on the groom's lap in Florencio's representation.

Other Mexican legends provided inspiration for Florencio. In 1989, he brought *La Llorona* (the Weeping Woman) to life in his tableau. According to the legend, she haunts waterways at night, wailing for her lost children (whom some say she drowned). It is common for parents to tell their youngsters not to play outside at night, especially around irrigation ditches and rivers, because *La Llorona* might get them. The mere mention of her name has the power to evoke terror in children.

Another grisly legendary character on exhibit was a life-size witch shown in her lair with her companions: rubber snakes, an inflated blow-up owl, and live morning doves in a cage (plate 4). In Mexico, some of the stories told about witches focus on the belief that they steal babies and drink their blood for nourishment. Florencio explained that when no babies can be found witches drink chickens' blood as a substitute. He placed the figure of a bloodied infant accompanied by two "dead" rubber chickens in a ceramic bowl beneath the witch in the tree to illustrate this detail.

Florencio blended fantasy with reality in

a way that incited fear in his audience. Obviously, the witch who took infants from their cribs and sucked their blood was fictitious, but her presence evoked the widespread anxiety all parents feel about the vulnerability of their young children. In 1990, he added another character who stole children, a green-faced, grinning hunchback holding a machete in one hand and a bloody baby in the other (plate 13). Carolina Morales pointed out that the kidnapping and selling of babies is in fact a problem in Mexico and recounted her own horrifying experience when an attempt was made to abduct her infant at a fiesta. Florencio's inclusion of this theme in the imaginary realm of his exhibit exemplifies his ability to provoke real fear in onlookers of all ages.

Florencio's constructions not only related to traditional Mexican stories and beliefs but also to his personal experiences. The treasure chest spilling over with gold and jewels (plate 14) is a reference to an encounter he had with a restless spirit while he was living with the old man. A few weeks after Florencio moved there, his sleep was disturbed by the sound of loud thumping footsteps coming from the kitchen. When he looked for the origin of the sounds, he could find nothing. However, one night he was awakened from a nightmare by the feeling of something or someone grabbing his ankle. He associated the sensation with the spirit of his landlord's recently deceased wife. During this encounter she told him of a buried treasure under the house which Florencio tried, but failed, to find.

Florencio drew attention to contemporary social issues by creating a cast of drunken characters surrounded by small mountains of whiskey, tequila, and beer bottles (plate 15). These pathetic characters were there to remind his audience to *"aprende a rechazar las drogas y apreciar la vida"* ("learn to refuse drugs and appreciate life"). Another vignette (plate 16) depicted a corpse in a shallow grave killed by *"los biles de la cantina"* ("the bar tabs") while yet another he called *"El Tequila"* (plate 17). Each of these miserable characters embodied a warning of the potential consequences of abusing drugs and alcohol. Perhaps Florencio's personal experience with his uncle's alcoholism motivated him to include these themes in his display.

Not every figure or scene alluded to a particular narrative or experience. In 1989, Florencio created a "tomb" adorned with Aztec and Spanish iconography. He framed a tombstone with two ceramic Indian god heads, decorated the burial mound below with strings of glittering beads, and thrust a large gilded sword deep into the dirt (plate 18). This historical interpretation illustrated Florencio's interest in the fall of the Aztec Empire at the hands of the Spanish conquistadors. Florencio took pride in his indigenous Mexican origins. The same tomb appeared in his 1990 Halloween display, but he added a bust of Michelangelo (plate 19). The assemblage no longer symbolized the demise of the Aztecs; instead it provided ambience for the richly decorated yard. Florencio said that the Michelangelo statue carried no particular meaning, that he put it there for visual effect just to draw attention. The ever-changing array afforded him the opportunity to express himself on a purely artistic level.

Florencio drew on diverse sources for inspiration. His art grew out of his experiences, both before and after he immigrated to the United States. In addition to incorporating many Mexican traditions, the Halloween yard assimilated images from American popular culture, including ghoulish bloody characters extracted from Hollywood gore movies; the result was a unique form of expression. After examining all the objects in the scene, Cristina Díaz offered this interpretation: "He lives in this culture but he came from a different one, and he's getting along living here with his background, so he's showing that in his yard. He's in the middle of two cultures, and he can get along very well with them."

This mixing of traditions could especially be seen in the way Florencio included elements in his Halloween exhibits from the Mexican customs surrounding the Day of the Dead. Two characters featured in the 1989 display differed from all the other pieces: the statues of John F. Kennedy (plate 20) and of Mr. Spock from "Star Trek." Florencio explained that Halloween occurs two days before the Mexican celebration of *El Día de los Muertos* (the Day of the Dead) November 2, when people pay their respects to the departed through elaborate rituals. In his Halloween yard, he was remembering these two personages. Mr. Spock stood for the first astronaut who "went to the stars." Florencio called attention to John F. Kennedy because "he was a great man, president, and symbol of this country." Cristina Díaz immediately understood why Florencio venerated Kennedy, explaining that Mexican Americans held J. F. K. in high esteem because he helped establish laws protecting and serving their interests. Florencio placed the bust of Kennedy amid a patch of carved jack-o'-lanterns and set up a torch similar to the "eternal flame" burning in Arlington Cemetery, Kennedy's burial place. Florencio pointed out that there was no blood around the statue, a demonstration of his respect for Kennedy.

Other components in the yard alluded to *El Día de los Muertos*. In the Halloween assemblage of 1990, Florencio added a significant item: an ornate altar to the dead that provided an isolated sanctuary from the gory scenes in the front yard (plate 9). In Mexico, making an altar for the dead during All Souls' Day is an important element in the series of rituals reserved for this occasion. Although traditional altars exhibit a large degree of individuality, they share the common element of food offerings. Often pictures of the deceased are placed upon the table. Florencio's altar, a long rectangular table offering an abundance of foods to the dead was set up at the end of the driveway and adjacent to his house. Carefully arranged bunches of grapes, apples, peaches, plums, red chilies, carrots and sweets, along with traditional sugar skulls, constituted the ritual feast. A forest of candles shed light on two chromolithographs of the Virgin of Guadalupe, foot-high statues of winged angels and other saints, and on two crucifixes placed in the center of the shrine. In front, a small pew provided a place for contemplation and prayer. Two illuminated jack-o'-lanterns flanked a hand-lettered sign that read, *"Por favor cooperen con el bill de la luz. El cielo gracias—Familia Morales"* ("Please help us pay our electricity bill. Thanks to the heavens—the Morales Family").

Other objects in the yard in 1989 and 1990 originated with Day of the Dead custom. Florencio's comical tombs resembled traditional graves in the way he constructed the simple wooden crosses and adorned them with flower wreaths. On *El Día de los Muertos* relatives renew their deceased loved ones' graves by cleaning them and the surrounding area and placing elaborate flower *coronas* (wreaths). Food and drink are brought to the cemetery to "feed" the deceased as well as the living. Florencio put half a squash on a platter on top of one of the burial mounds in his display as well as various treasures and glittering objects probably representing *offrendas* (offerings) to the dead (plate 16). Carolina Morales saw the connection. "When he began [decorating for] Halloween he mixed what is here in the United States with what is over there [in Mexico]. Over there, there are towns where on the Day of the Dead they adorn the tombstones with paper, with flowers, and with food as an offering. At night they go to the tombstones—and I believe that he put the tombstones up a bit satirically, taking something from over there and mixing it with masks from here."

Both Halloween and *El Día de los Muertos* are occasions when trickery and parody prevail. In Mexico the Day of the Dead provides a time to reflect upon, but also to make fun of, death. The *calavera** (skull) commonly symbolizes death in a farcical light. Sculpted skeletons engage in everyday activities appearing as mariachi musicians, as people riding a packed bus, or as farmers harvesting a crop. Florencio also included a traditional life-size papier maché *calavera* in his display (plate 3). "The common saying *'A mí la muerte me pela los*

* *Calaca* may also be used as a synonym for *calavera* (skull). *Calaveras* and *calacas*, by extension, refer to the satirical broadsheets featuring mock epitaphs for the living circulated on the Day of the Dead. A third meaning of calavera applies on this occasion when children (and, in the past, adults) ask for *calaveras*, gifts of money and/or fruit.

dientes' (literally: death makes me peel my teeth = laugh) is telling of the close, humorous relationship Mexicans have with *la pelona* (the bald one)," writes Stellweg (1988:19).

Florencio mocked death in many of his yard installations. Cristina Díaz said that Florencio's placards in the form of epitaphs reminded her of the humorous rhyming poems people compose about friends, family or public figures. In the schools, children post these verses on the walls. The editorial pages of Mexican newspapers print *calacas* (literally "death figures") that humorously describe the imaginary deaths of prominent people in Mexican society; no one is spared, not even the clergy or political heads. Sometimes these poems are illustrated with caricatures of the people as skeletons. Carolina Morales offered an example. "For my son I would write that he died because he was mischievous and stubborn, and Death took him and now he's resting in hallowed ground. But only people who hold each other in esteem and who know each other very well [exchange verses], so that they don't take it personally. They write, 'Death took him because of his mischief' or whatever [suits] the defect or characteristic of the person in question. Or if he's a dancer, they say he's dancing in hallowed ground with Death."

In one case, Florencio incorporated a *calaca* in his display. He erected a statue of a pirate raising a gilded cup to his mouth and brandishing a large knife in the other hand (plate 17). The accompanying sign exclaimed, *"R.I.P. Aquí yace Tiburcio 'El Tequila,' el terrorífico matón"* ("R.I.P. Here lies Tiburcio 'Tequila,' the terrifying killer"). Tiburcio was one of the Moraleses' neighbors from Mexico described by Florencio's family as a drunkard and a womanizer who became belligerent when intoxicated. Florencio's comical portrayal fits the genre of the *calaca* because Tiburcio was still alive, and Florencio focused on the actual defects of the man's character to account for his alleged death. He exaggerated Tiburcio's explosive anger to the point that the man became a "killer," thereby incorporating Tiburcio into the cast of deadly characters in Florencio's display. In another epitaph placed next to a corpse in a grave, Florencio used the rhyme and verse of the *calaca: "Aquí yace y yace bien, él descansa y yo también"* ("Here he lies resting well, he rests in peace and I as well").

Florencio was noted for his sense of humor. "When he went in any shop or a secretary's office, and if she was sad or serious, he would come and joke around with her," said Alfonso Morales. "They knew him as a joker. When they already knew him [they would say] 'Oh, there's Mr. Morales. Let's see what he has to say now.' He told them jokes and they laughed and laughed." The celebration of Halloween allowed Florencio to express this aspect of his personality. In addition to engaging his audience through his comic impersonation of Count Dracula, he incorporated humor in nearly all of the scenes in his display (plate 21).

Comical elements are obvious in such details as the cigar-chomping werewolf (plate 15) and in the male/female character in a cobweb-sheathed coffin, sword driven through the heart (plate 22). The sign on the latter read *"R.I.P. Aquí reposa El 'Siete Machos,' lo mató . . . su marido"* ("Here lies the seven times macho, his husband killed him"). According to Florencio, *El Siete Machos,* a famous character known for his machismo, had seven girlfriends (at least), but also a male lover. When his boyfriend discovered *El Siete's* entourage of women, he killed him in a jealous rage. When Florencio retold this story both he and a bystander burst into laughter. To understand the humorous aspect of his representation, the taboo of homosexuality, especially for Latinos, must be considered. Florencio poked fun by inverting and discrediting the prevailing Mexican concept of masculinity embodied by the macho man.

Many scholars studying festive behavior have focused on symbolic inversions. At festival time the world is turned upside-down, and participants may cross-dress or act in ways they would never consider in the context of everyday existence. In addition to creating *El Siete Machos,* Florencio reversed other social conventions to call attention to their importance. Murderers, alcoholics, drug addicts and evildoers dominated his tableaux. The use of these reversals in the Halloween display enabled Florencio to indicate and affirm the deepest moral and social values of the community.

Florencio expressed his personal standards by depicting a miser staring ruefully from his grave at the wealth he had accumulated during his life (plate 23). Carolina Morales explained, "It's the story of a person who does nothing but save his money and doesn't let anyone touch his money. He doesn't give anything to anybody. And when he dies he doesn't have anyone to give it to. And the people around him aren't interested, they prefer to have friendships and to experience an inner life. That's all very superficial, the money and all that, right? So, they say, 'Well, now he's dead and he never enjoyed his riches because he was hoarding it all.'" Her husband, Alfonso, pointed out that Florencio buried the miser looking at the jewels so that he could guard his money in the afterlife. This character's actions provided a stark contrast to Florencio's generosity as exemplified by the pleasure he gave to others through his holiday exhibits and the grand fiesta on All Hallows' Eve.

Besides highlighting many of the paradoxes of life and death, Florencio dealt with other contradictions such as the deterioration of the family resulting from drug and alcohol abuse. Many of the scenes in the Halloween yard revolved around this theme.

Honoring of deceased family members on the Day of the Dead reinforces the high value Mexicans and Mexican Americans place on the institution of the family. The fact that Florencio's entire extended family, including his mother, resided in Teoloyucan made contact difficult and rare. He often lamented their absence. By obligation, the living must go to the nearest family cemetery plot and ritually renew the space by repainting the grave marker, arranging fresh flowers, replacing old wreaths with new ones, and clearing away any debris in the area. Since it was impractical to travel deep into Mexico to the burial sites of his family, Florencio symbolically enacted the ritual in his front yard. When he added the altar to his assemblage, he fulfilled his responsibility to venerate and honor the dead. Perhaps a major reason that Florencio made such a monumental effort to extend his hospitality to the entire neighborhood and beyond sprang from his lack of ties in Los Angeles and the high value he attached to family and community. Creating the yard assemblage was an attempt to resolve his paradox in a novel way.

Paul Jenkins, who lived in an apartment complex a few doors away from Florencio, said that he thought the yard displays and associated festivities curbed crime in the neighborhood. "To the south and the west there is a great deal of gang activity and it doesn't seem to penetrate around here. Perhaps in some way his presence and the presence of his *compadres* has something to do with that. Many people have guard devices and dogs around here; he doesn't seem to need it. It would be a rare occurrence if someone would try to burgle him, or cause him harm." Jenkins mentioned that the huge party Morales held on Halloween night provided an important family-oriented alternative to the dangerous exploits of hooliganism one hears about on this occasion.

However, during the week preceding Halloween, as his exhibit neared completion, Florencio slept outside on a mattress in the bed of his truck so he could guard his yard. On a couple of occasions neighborhood youth did steal the mechanical hands Florencio had attached to some of the corpses buried in the graves. Another time someone took the figure of Death. Despite these thefts, Florencio tried to create an atmosphere of trust and mutual responsibility. To help defray his expenses he placed a tray in the center of his installation along with a sign requesting contributions (plate 15). Sometimes he let the donations accrue for a few days before he emptied the platter. One time some local schoolchildren stole the unattended money. When their teacher found out, she notified Florencio and made the young thieves admit their guilt and return their booty. This event illustrated Florencio's importance in the community and the feelings of responsibility toward him.

Florencio received a great deal of attention as a result of his displays. Reporters came out in force to cover his Halloween creations. In 1991, KMEX (Channel 34) featured the yard on local television and made the tape available through a network feed for national broadcast. Most of his neighbors deeply appreciated his efforts. Paul Jenkins said, "It makes it more of a neighborhood than I think it would be were it not for him. Unfortunately we all live in isolation these days and he sort of takes the curse off that." A few dissenters did not approve of Florencio's installation. The local Jehovah's Witnesses sent a delegation to see Florencio to evaluate his motives. He laughed as he explained, "Even the brothers came to pray for me so I won't go to hell. No really, they've come. They told me on Halloween, 'We want to rescue you from the hands of the devil.'" Florencio felt they didn't understand his good intentions so in 1990 he erected a sign stating, *"Estas escenas sangrientas son pura diversión. No tienen nada que ver con nuestras creencias religiosas—Familia Morales"* ("These bloody scenes are only for amusement. They have no relation to our religious beliefs—the Morales Family").

Perhaps the greatest and most personal dilemma Florencio tackled in the 1990 Halloween yard was that of his own death. Just one month earlier he had learned he had lung cancer. Although he did manage to erect the display again in 1991 with the help of his brother Alberto, he thought that his exhibit in 1990 would be his last. The sign Florencio wrote and placed beneath the life-size papier maché skeleton in the 1990 yard read, "You too, will be like me."

Christmas

Second to Halloween, Florencio considered his Christmas display (plate 24) to be the most important of the year. In Florencio's *nacimiento* the Holy Family and Wise Men occupied the central area of the *ramada* (arbor) (plate 26). Numerous animals including sheep, camels, cows, and *burros* lay in the straw surrounding the religious personages with ceramic angels bordering the scene. The figures ranged from two feet to about five feet tall; many were internally illuminated. A large picture of the Virgin of Guadalupe hung on the back wall of the shelter (plate 25). Green, white and red bows (the Mexican national colors) graced her presence. The elephant-leaf philodendron plants provided a naturalistic backdrop for the Holy Birth. On the right edge of the *ramada* stood a plastic electric Winnie-the-Pooh bear in Christmas garb (plate 29). A real Christmas tree more than ten feet high, richly decorated and sprayed with "snow," appeared on the left. A second depiction of the Virgin of Guadalupe hung on the front of the structure surrounded by glittering gold streamers and white lights. On the roof of the house a flashy gold Christmas tree was flanked by two carolers and an additional two Wise Men. Two American flags, one on each side, danced high in the breeze. Christmas music filled the air, coming from speakers built into the large *ramada.* The effect of this electrical masterpiece was overwhelming. Flashing colored lights outlined the trees and *ramada.* Electrical signs proclaiming *"Viva México"* and *"Feliz Navidad"* twinkled from above.

Over a ten-year period beginning in 1981, Florencio added more items to his *nacimiento,* the ultimate goal being to fill the space completely. Sometimes people donated decorations. Once two men driving by stopped when they saw his nativity scene. Impressed, they offered to give Florencio some large figures for his display, which he promptly accepted. Florencio was zealous about his Christmas exhibit. His sky-high electrical bills, easily five-hundred dollars for the month of December, did not deter him.

Creating the *nacimiento* took a month. At the end of November, Florencio began building the large-scale *ramada* to house the nativity. By the end of the first week of December, admirers found the display breathtaking. Florencio said, however, "Right now, it is ugly to me." His satisfaction came only after he had filled the yard with decorations on a monumental scale. In 1989, Florencio waited to add the final touches until December 13. At that time he completed the assemblage by planting many varieties of aloe vera and cacti, as well as poinsettias, in front of the *ramada.* He also added more lights after installing a new circuit breaker to compensate for the excess electricity. The display could not be completed until December 13 because a Mass would be held in his yard on December 12, and the congregation of his church would occupy the empty space in front of the *ramada.*

Every year, beginning in the mid-1980's, Florencio invited the priest of his church to conduct Mass on that date, the feast day of the Virgin of Guadalupe. Florencio maintained close ties with the priests of Sacred Heart Roman Catholic Church in Montebello. Alfonso Morales said, "Florencio told them one year in advance, 'Father, write it down in advance for next year.'" The whole congregation of Florencio's church came to his yard annually to commemorate "Our Lady."

The Virgin of Guadalupe is the object of widespread religious veneration in Mexico. According to legend, just after the conquest in 1531, she appeared to an Indian named Juan Diego on a hill called Tepeyac, sacred to the Aztec goddess Tonantzín

("Our Mother"). She told Juan Diego to tell the bishop that she wanted a church built on that spot. When Juan Diego recounted his experience the bishop did not believe the story. Juan Diego returned to the spot where she reappeared and insisted that he try again. When he attempted to convince the bishop a second time, he was told not to return unless he could bring a token from the Virgin. The next day the Virgin appeared to Juan Diego and told him to go to the place on the hill where he had first seen her and pick some roses, which would serve as evidence to the bishop. He obeyed and found beautiful Castilian roses where previously only cacti had grown. He placed these in his *tilma* (cape) and went to the bishop's palace, where the servants saw the roses. When they tried to take one, the flowers became part of his cape. This time the bishop believed Juan Diego, recognizing the sign from the Virgin. When Juan Diego opened his cape to give a rose to the bishop, the image of the Virgin materialized on his *tilma.* After that the bishop built the church, and converts came by the thousands to worship her.

The Virgin of Guadalupe's image pervades popular culture throughout Mexico and also in Mexican American communities. She commonly appears on *barrio* murals, car ornaments, religious candles, and T-shirts. Not only a representation of Mary, the mother of God, the Virgin of Guadalupe is the symbolic mother of all Mexicans. By hosting the Mass to commemorate *La Guadalupana,* Florencio demonstrated his respect and honor in a unique way.

Besides providing the sacred space for the celebration of Our Lady, Florencio hosted *Las Posadas,* a widely practiced Mexican tradition that takes place on the nine nights before Christmas. It consists of a procession of singing travelers who represent Joseph and Mary seeking shelter in Bethlehem. The word *posada* literally means shelter. On each night a candlelight procession walks along the streets, stopping at numerous prearranged houses to ask for refuge. They are refused until they reach the final designated house where the doors open wide and the company within welcomes the weary pilgrims with song. The accompanying fiesta includes seasonal Christmas foods such as tamales, hot chocolate and pastries, and the breaking of piñatas. The participants place the statues of Mary and Joseph on a specially prepared altar where they rest until the next evening, when they start again on their way. On the ninth night, Christmas Eve, the final stop of *Las Posadas* is usually the parish church.

In 1988, *Las Posadas* ended at Florencio's house on Christmas Eve. As the pilgrims sang outside, an electrical fuse blew, and the lights went out. Florencio lamented not being able to restore the power and so he took special precautions in 1989 by installing an extra power box outside to handle the excessive wattage. His fiesta in 1988 without lights was not a failure, however, and everyone remained to sing, eat, drink and break piñatas. Florencio said the priest told him not to break all the piñatas and to save some for the church. "No problem, Father." They smashed five piñatas at his house and broke two more at the church. "Piñatas are very important. Without piñatas, there's no *Posadas,*" said Florencio.

In addition to providing the locale for some of the formally enacted aspects of Mexican Christmas ritual, Florencio's *nacimiento* served as an informal place for people to socialize and experience the spirituality of the holiday. Many passing cars slowed or stopped every evening during the Christmas season, and families strolled by to visit the shrine (plate 28). Most people stood by the low iron fence quietly reflecting on the scene; the aesthetic response seemed too overpowering for words. A few passersby congratulated Florencio on his work. One evening while Florencio was outside, a Columbian named Edgar introduced himself. He said he had driven from Pasadena especially to see the *nacimiento* because in Columbia they also erect nativity scenes in their homes. His mother had taught him to make them, and that year he had created a small nativity scene in his apartment. Edgar told Florencio that all of his family resided in Columbia, and he was alone in the United States. He said that his mother had come to visit him here: "She was here one month, then she had a heart attack and passed away. She was a very smart lady, too, and very creative." Seeing Florencio's *nacimiento* had opened up a vivid stream of memories for Edgar. He volunteered to help the Catholic church distribute free food to needy families, and he gave the Morales family a large case of strawberries and many heads of lettuce as a token of his appreciation. This exchange between Edgar, previously a stranger, and the Moraleses demonstrates that the creation of the *nacimiento* provided a setting for the members of the community, from both near and far, to interact personally and spiritually.

Florencio's exhibit had other consequences. "Before Florencio began putting up the *nacimiento,* nobody put up lights in the windows," said Carolina. "It was very sad. When he put up his *nacimiento* and lights in the trees, the rest of the people began adorning their windows." Florencio explained that his greatest reward was "when the people smile, I don't need the newspaper, I don't need the T.V." Florencio, always modest about the attention he received, declared, "It's for everybody, it's not only for me. It's too heavy for me, only for me."

Assembling nativity scenes has been a

Christmas tradition in the western world for centuries. "Legend ascribes the first such assemblage to St. Francis of Assisi, whose devotion to the Christ Child is a matter of historical record" (Griffith, 1988:118). In Mexico, Christians erected simple nativity scenes as early as the 1500s. By the 1700s, both church and home displayed expanded sets. The distinctive Mexican *nacimiento* incorporates scenes from the Old and New Testaments as well as from Mexican rural life. Individual families may depict the Holy Birth with a small group of miniature figures. More elaborate home scenes may cover the entire corner of a room, incorporating hundreds of figures and featuring a landscaped setting with live plants, mosses, and running water.

Florencio's *nacimiento,* conventional in the depiction of the Holy Birth, departed from tradition in the matter of size. Rather than featuring miniature characters in the corner of a room, Florencio used extremely large figures, which he placed outdoors. He explained that one would see a display similar to his inside a church in Mexico. "All the churches do them." Alfonso Morales pointed out that "they use smaller figures. In some places they use large figures, in large churches, but they're usually not that big." Alfonso's wife Carolina added, "Yes, it's a little bit similar. Of course, Florencio had a bigger space to work with." In fact, his local church requested his help and creative input in the making of displays to commemorate different holy days during the year.

Florencio's deep religious faith inspired him to make the extravagant Christmas tableau. For him the *nacimiento* functioned both as an expression of his religion and as a fulfillment of an obligation to God and to the Virgin of Guadalupe. As he explained, "I made a promise to finish this, to not forget—to God, to the Virgin—three years ago—to fix my papers [for a work permit]. At that time, sometime around Christmas, they [government officials] were supposed to either approve or reject me. I thought to myself, 'Oh, God, I'm not a crook or anything, and of course they'll accept me. But on the other hand, I've been working under someone else's name and they won't accept me.' And meanwhile I was working alone here thinking, 'Oh, dear Virgin, help me. Don't think that when I arrange all my papers that I will forget everything. I'll continue to do it like I'm doing it now, and if I have more, I'll make it bigger still. And I'll continue doing it as long as I can.'" In 1985, Florencio received his working papers from the United States government, and partly as a result of his *manda* (vow) to the Virgin, he continued to display and expand the *nacimiento* until his death.

Florencio's enormous *nacimiento* announced his piety to the public, thus serving a purpose that is similar to that of the

Mexican American *capillas* (small chapels or yard shrines) that are constructed in front yards facing outward to catch the gaze of passersby. In both cases, the religious shrines demonstrate that a gift from God has been reciprocated with a gift to God.

Ties to his family provided another inducement for Florencio's display. During the Christmas season in 1989, he made another vow when erecting the nativity. He said, "Now I'm worried about my mother who is sick. She has hypertension. And I said to myself, 'Crying won't do any good. May God protect her, and I have to continue doing what I do.'" He explained that many people become self-absorbed during their depressions. He felt that it was more productive to focus his energy on creating the *nacimiento* and on what it represented. In addition to proclaiming faith in God, the display provided a therapeutic outlet, enabling him through the artistic process to relieve his anxiety and depression about his mother's sickness.

In constructing the grandiose display, Florencio also sought to re-create the sense of community and family ties that are affirmed during Christmas celebrations. In Mexico these holiday festivities encompass most of the months of December and January, ending on February 2 with *El Día de la Candeleria* (Candlemas). The pageantry and ritual range from the processions of *Las Posadas* to the making of a *nacimiento* in the family home. Florencio began to make his exhibits on Griffin Avenue more elaborate in the early 1980s when he could not return to Mexico as often because of responsibilities to his own family in Los Angeles. He felt isolated during the Christmas season because he could not join his extended family. "Everybody is in Mexico, brothers, sisters, parents. Because of that I get nostalgic. Over there we do large things like this and celebrate with spirit. Coming to this country—Well, one cries from sadness because he is not accustomed to it."

Other Holidays

In addition to the elaborate Christmas and Halloween assemblages, other holidays were recognized in Florencio's exhibits as well. Some years he added new fetes or modified his existing repertoire according to his artistic sensibilities. He also omitted installations for some holidays he had celebrated earlier. During the last two years of his life his illness and long hospital stays prevented him from fabricating particular displays.

Florencio selected a diversity of festivities encompassing many themes. For Easter he erected three large wooden crosses in the yard as an expression of his deep religious convictions (plate 30). On the largest central cross, an abstract representation of Christ's crucifixion, he placed a symbolic crown of red lights, which he illuminated at night.

On Valentine's Day Florencio made a gigantic red heart by constructing an internal frame, covering it with red satin material, and stuffing it to give it dimension. He then placed the heart in the center of his yard (plate 31). Blinking red lights bordered the massive sculpture. In 1990 he placed four vertical red, white and blue banners on both sides of the heart and tied giant red bows to the fence. The electric "*Viva México*" sign, resurrected from the Christmas display, crowned the roof. The ever-present flags of the United States, California and Mexico completed the display. In 1991, Florencio modified and expanded this exhibit by placing a newly fabricated heart between huge American and Mexican flags (plate 32). Each year on February 14, couples arrived at the yard to have their pictures taken in front of the giant heart. The Moraleses and other neighbors set up a table in the driveway where they sold flowers and homemade ornaments for people to buy as gifts for their special valentines.

Florencio paid similar homage to Mother's Day. He used the red heart as the centerpiece and filled the surrounding area with flowers. He further celebrated by bringing bouquets to his favorite clients and family members. On Mother's Day of 1988, one of the priests from Sacred Heart Roman Catholic Church conducted a Mass in his yard. He had always observed both Mother's Day and Valentine's Day in Mexico and continued to celebrate these occasions in the United States, expressing love for family and friends in both locales.

Florencio also devised constructions for important Mexican civic holidays. For *Cinco de Mayo,* he commissioned the brother of his sister-in-law, Mauro Ramírez Toreces, to paint a special mural on canvas (plate 33). It depicts the Mexican victory over the French at the Battle of Puebla on the fifth of May in 1862. In the center of the canvas, a bare-chested Indian represents Lucas, who headed the native *Zacapoaxtlas* (Aztec) forces, holding the Mexican flag. Beneath him on the right the French army marches under their flag and fires cannons aimed at the Mexicans. The Mexican commander, General Ignacio Zaragoza (on the left), leads the army. His troops consist of common men and women who have only rifles with which to confront the French. Although the French were not ousted until five years later, the Battle of Puebla has lasting meaning as the symbolic end of French intervention, and of the courageous defense of Mexico against foreign rule.

Other symbols of Mexican national pride on this occasion included tall green, white and red vertical banners framing the Mexican flag above the mural (plate 34). The flashing "*Viva México*" sign reinforced this theme. Florencio also incorporated

American flags and four star-spangled banners as a reminder of his dual patriotism. He said he always celebrated by hosting a barbecue in his yard for friends and family.

The exhibit for Mexican Independence Day (plate 35) resembled that of *Cinco de Mayo.* Pleased by the first mural, he asked Mauro Ramírez to paint a second canvas, this time commemorating Mexican Independence Day. This mural features three of the heroes who fought for an independent Mexico: Josefina Ortíz de Domínguez, Father Hidalgo, and José María Morelos y Pavón. Florencio placed a huge plaster sculpture of the Aztec calendar (about eight feet in diameter) painted in vibrant colors below the Independence Day canvas (plates 35 and 36). It further evoked the culture and power of the indigenous people who took up arms against the oppressive colonial government. Florencio said that his clients at *Plaza de la Raza,* a Chicano arts and cultural center in East Los Angeles, gave him the sculpture when he worked there as a gardener. He and a friend revitalized it by applying an undercoat of white and painting the relief forms in eye-catching colors. This time he placed the "*Viva México*" sign on top of the Aztec calendar and planted a variety of cacti and aloe veras around the base of this ancient symbol to create an authentic setting for the tableau. Oversize Mexican and United States flags provided a colorful and evocative backdrop for the sculpture. To pay homage to the women who fought for the country's independence, Florencio added a department store mannequin wearing a traditional embroidered dress and carrying a rifle to represent a *soldadera* (female soldier).

Florencio continuously sought ways to improve and expand his exhibits. Dissatisfied with his initial Mexican Independence Day display, Florencio asked Mauro Ramírez to paint him a larger canvas for this occasion. The new canvas, featured in 1989, is not only more grandiose but also illustrates the historical events leading up to Mexican independence from Spain (plate 36).

Father Hidalgo, a priest in the town of Dolores, empathized with the Indians and the oppression they suffered. He attained heroic status throughout Mexico by initiating the revolt that resulted in an independent Mexico in 1821. On the morning of September 16, 1810, Hidalgo and his townspeople arrested all the Spaniards in town. After ringing the church bells, as if summoning the Indians to Mass, he stood in the pulpit and announced that it was time to throw off the yoke of Spanish control. Then Hidalgo gave the legendary *grito de Dolores* (outcry from Dolores): "*¡Viva Nuestra Señora de Guadalupe! Viva la Independencia!*" ("Long live Our Lady of Guadalupe! Long live Independence!"). A few days later in Atotonilco, near Guadalajara, Hidalgo seized a banner of the

Virgin of Guadalupe and led them in their fight. The Virgin became the symbol of inspiration for the insurgents.

The new Independence Day mural graphically represents these events. Two large clenched fists, chained together in the center of the canvas, symbolize the Spaniards' domination of the native people. A chisel driven through the chain serves to break the oppressing force and liberate the hands. A large, flat, blood-red area separates them from the rest of the scene. The main actors in the top portion of the mural carry their simple weapons, axes and machetes, on their way to conquer the Spanish. Father Miguel Hidalgo y Costillo stands in the center of this grouping, holding a yellow banner bearing the image of the Virgin of Guadalupe. Large ringing church bells sound out above them. A message in the lower right hand corner reads, *"Por una patria libre e independiente—México 1810"* ("For a free and independent fatherland—Mexico 1810").

The murals for *Cinco de Mayo* and September 16 suited Florencio's needs because they were graphic representations of historical events he deemed important. By placing the murals in his front yard, he drew public attention to Mexican history and culture, subjects he held dear. When people stopped and asked him about these exhibits, he used the murals as didactic tools in recounting the historical events.

The new canvas commemorating September 16 includes the three instigating forces of social action that led to Mexico's independence: Hidalgo, "the Father of the Motherland"; *el grito,* the call to battle which reverberated throughout the country; and the Virgin of Guadalupe, who represented the Aztec goddess to the Indians and Christ's mother to the Spaniards. These emblems evoke cultural pride during the celebrations held in observance of this holiday in Mexico and the United States. In Mexico City, just before midnight on September 15, the president stands on the balcony of the National Palace and gives the *grito* to the populace below and then rings a small, very old bell (reportedly the one from the church at Dolores). This signals widespread rejoicing throughout the country; bells, horns and whistles sound and fireworks explode. The following day's celebrations include military parades, concerts and various ceremonies.

Florencio's festivities in 1991 consisted of a church Mass and party held in his yard on the eve of September 16. He advertised the event to the public through a large handmade sign crowned with a cross that read, *"15 de setiembre—8 de la noche—Misa y grito de la independencia"* ("September 15—8 p.m.—Mass and the outcry of independence"). His church congregation, friends and neighbors turned out in great numbers. After the formal Mass, Florencio, as the official host of the celebration, gave a speech extolling the importance of the holiday and then launched the party with a reenactment of the historic *grito de Dolores.* Everyone stayed to eat, dance, and converse. Florencio explained that in the past he had taken his family downtown to the large civic celebration, which featured live music and Mexican food. One year some drunk gang members caused a fight, killing an innocent bystander, and he stopped attending. Instead of risking danger, he provided a safe place for his family and friends to gather in celebration of this significant Mexican and Mexican American holiday.

Florencio also drew attention to a lesser-known civic holiday, the anniversary of the Treaty of Teoloyucan, celebrated on August 13. Although few Americans know of this historic day, Florencio felt the need for observance not only because the events occurred in his home town, but also because it signified the end of the Mexican Revolution. Carolina Morales explained that many Mexicans know of it because it is taught to schoolchildren in classes in Mexican history. She said, "The signing of the treaty was very important. When the treaty was signed there were people from Brazil, from Guatemala, from France, from Italy. They were there as witnesses. The treaty was between the government army and the revolutionaries. That was when the army agreed to receive the revolutionaries, who were led at the time by Alvaro Obregón. And they signed the treaty regarding the establishment of the presidency and they agreed on how they would withdraw the armed forces." Florencio did not feature this holiday between 1989 and 1992, and therefore I never had the opportunity to witness the display. He did commemorate it in 1988, according to a newspaper article of that year.

Florencio included uniquely American holidays in his festive cycle as well. For Thanksgiving (plate 37), a life-size mannequin dressed as a chef engaged in the preparation of a Thanksgiving feast (plate 38). Florencio comically posed the gourmet in the act of decapitating the "turkey" (a recycled rubber chicken from the Halloween display). Behind him stood a mythical tree of life from which a proliferation of plastic fruits and vegetables "grew." On a banquet table in front, the chef offered an abundance of fruits, liquors, and festive foods. A wide swath of red, white and blue fabric bordered the periphery of the yard, in addition to the four vertical banners that carried these colors. At night, torches and floodlights illuminated the display. Florencio used the Thanksgiving exhibit as an opportunity to express American patriotism in a dramatic medium. He also hosted a large dinner for his friends and family. George Rivera and Juan Esteves, who grew up on this street, said that they remembered a Thanksgiving when Florencio held a feast in the front yard. He invited all his neighbors and set up a long banquet table in the driveway.

On Memorial Day Florencio created a simulated United States military cemetery in his yard by constructing and erecting numerous wooden grave markers (plate 39). He evoked the ceremony of a soldier's burial by displaying a mock casket enshrouded by a flag. The Stars and Stripes provided a bold central backdrop while more modest Mexican and American flags were planted diagonally on each side of the installation.

For the Fourth of July Florencio wrapped a large red, white and blue banner around the entire yard. He placed the American flag centrally, flanking it with other vertical banners. The exhibit featured a six-foot-tall sculpture of the Statue of Liberty, which was elevated on a table. One of Florencio's favorite experiences on this holiday occurred when a woman, *"una Americana,"* visited the yard. He said, "She came by on the Fourth of July and stopped to look at all the flags and the exhibit. 'Someone really important must live here,' she said. 'Maybe an ambassador.' I told her that I didn't really know. I'm just the gardener" (as quoted in the *Los Angeles Times,* Boyer, 1988).

Influences, Aesthetics, and Style

Florencio derived much satisfaction from his displays because his art afforded him a way to express his personality. Family members pointed out that he had always been a leader and an extrovert. As a teenager in Mexico, he took great pleasure in organizing parties and sports-related activities. Carolina Morales said, "He always liked to be the head, the leader, to organize everything." Alfonso Morales explained, "He was the one who organized us." As a young man, Florencio initiated and coordinated a local soccer team in Teoloyucan. Since no adequate playing field existed, he took it upon himself to create one. He used the money he had earned and encouraged the players to pitch in, too. Alfonso said that Florencio also solicited funds from the more affluent ranchers in the community. "He said to them, 'Help our team. We're making a playing field that will look beautiful in our neighborhood.' And they helped him. He paid the workers to bring grass and plant it. And then he had goals [installed] and huts built from palm fronds on each side of the field with benches for the players. It looked pretty. He always found a way to raise money to pay the referees and the league."

Florencio did not limit himself to organizing team sports; he also took pleasure in planning parties. As a teenager, he staged celebratory activities during Halloween. In a custom similar to trick or treating in the United States, people in Mexico go out and ask for the *calavera* and receive money and/or fruits. His brother, Alfonso, recalled that "he got us together, a group, he would say, 'Let's go ask for the *calavera.* Let's go get the keys to the church; we'll be in charge of ringing.' They play the church bells on October 31; they ring the church bells all night long. He would say, 'You guys go to the church; you guys go trick or treating,' and he would send everyone somewhere. Asking for the *calavera,* they gave you money and fruit, and they all came back with their fruit, and they split it between everyone. They ate it all. They ate the fruit, the bread, and later, they put the money together to see how much they had. Then Florencio would say, 'O.K. You go buy some sodas, or wine, or beer.' And they would spend the whole night until dawn playing around and joking. It's very beautiful all that, to have a *lunada"* (moonlight party). Alfonso suggested that this early love of celebrating important occasions later inspired the holiday assemblages. "From there he could have gotten a lot of that spirit. He had a lot of imagination. Little by little, it was born within him."

The art in Florencio's surroundings played a formative role in his later creations. According to a report in the *Los Angeles Times* (Boyer, 1988), Florencio said, "As a child, whenever I would go to Mexico City, I would see large, floodlit displays. I thought to myself that one day, when I'm able, I'll do something similar."

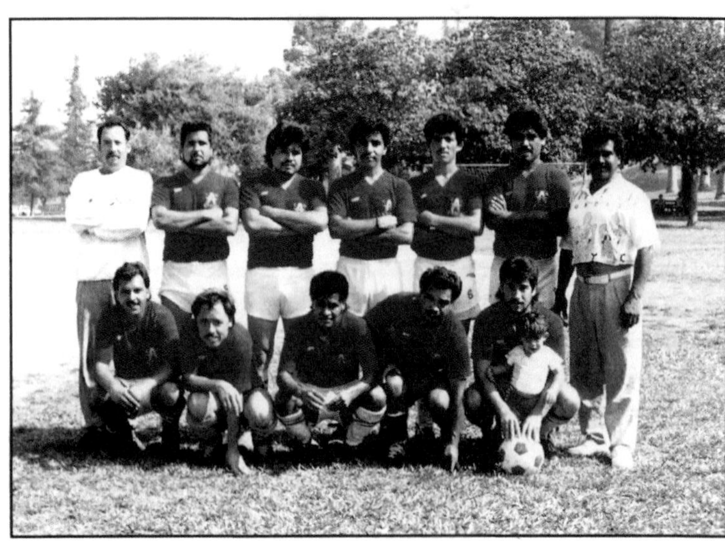

Florencio Morales (standing, far right) with his Abraham Lincoln Soccer League team in Los Angeles (circa 1985). Florencio owned the team and also served as secretary of the league for two years.

After Florencio left Mexico and came to work in the United States, his new experiences and environment affected his art. He expressed his identity as an immigrant and his occupation as a gardener in his holiday exhibits. In the displays reserved for Mexican holidays he always incorporated the American flag, just as he included Mexican flags in the installations associated with uniquely American festivities. Halloween, as well as other celebrations, provided the opportunity to combine Mexican and American themes. Cristina Díaz said, "He's doing it because it has something to do with his Mexican traditions. See, he's showing you what Mexicans do for *El Día de los Muertos,* but at the same time he doesn't want to leave out the American tradition because he is living in this country."

Florencio also used his skills and resources as a gardener. He completely replanted the foreground of his *nacimiento* with cacti, aloe vera plants and poinsettias. He often resodded the grass and altered the landscape of the front yard to create effects for his displays. He also saved all cuttings from exotic plants to use in enhancing his constructions.

In each of the holiday yards an underlying aesthetic of richness of detail and of dramatic contrasts predominated. Florencio assembled elements from diverse contexts to create a lucid and meaningful whole. Carolina Morales pointed out that he liked to put unrelated symbols and materials side by side to make a contrast, "to give it more *salsa*" (zest). In the Halloween display, the framing of a bust of Michelangelo by two Aztec icons was to Florencio both dramatic and beautiful.

"Assembling bits and pieces" has been called "the stylistic basis of the Mexican American folk aesthetic" (Seriff and Limón, 1986: 40), although it can be found in works of folk art outside this ethnic group. James S. Griffith refers to this aesthetic as a "Baroque principle of organization," (1987:15) drawing a connection between the eighteenth-century Mexican baroque style of architecture and twentieth-century Mexican American folk art. He explains: "To treat these modes of organization as direct survivals from the 18th century would be in my view putting the cart before the horse. It seems much more likely that both they and the style of architectural decoration we call Baroque are results of a set of rules—a sense of how things should go together—that has been a part of Mexican culture since at least the 18th century." Griffith points out that the baroque style of decoration employs dramatic contrasts in painting and architecture. Artists achieve contrasts by juxtaposing plain and decorated surfaces, utilizing many colors, and creating light and dark areas. He stresses that "richness," a hallmark of the baroque style, includes "richness of material, of texture and of detail and content." In addition, the individual aspects of decoration in Mexican baroque architecture are "made up of totally independent entities each of which has its own meaning." Griffith demonstrates that these same principles operate in the Mexican American community of artists who create low riders, yard shrines and grave markers.

Metaphorically speaking, Florencio's holiday yards have a "baroque" quality. For Halloween, he combined a religious altar, a bust of John F. Kennedy, and a figure of Satan hovering above. In the Christmas yard, electric lights and glittering surfaces excited the eye and added contrast to the holy figures below in the hay. A Winnie-the-Pooh bear wearing a Santa cap stood next to the scene of the Holy Birth. Florencio verbalized the concept of the baroque aesthetic when he said that completely filling the space of his yard was his artistic goal. As he repeated themes from one year to the next his compositions grew increasingly complex (compare plates 31 and 32, and plates 35 and 36).

In terms of form, Florencio's displays did not look like everyday domestic yard decor. Many of his viewers commented that they had never seen anything quite like his exhibits, especially the array for Halloween. However, Americans commonly choose to adorn the spaces around their homes for holidays, especially Christmas, when decorations often include nativity scenes, Santas, and colored lights. In all regions of the United States, individuals carve jack-o'-lanterns to place in a window or on a front stoop for Halloween. Some even erect representations of monsters, ghosts and devils outside their homes or go as far as making a "haunted house" for neighborhood kids. Florencio's displays embodied these holiday decorating traditions. Although some people may decorate for holidays on the same scale as Florencio, usually their repertoire is limited to a few special holidays. Florencio's art, both in scale and subject, also resembles the types of displays one finds on view in public places for important nationally celebrated holidays.

Florencio curated his exhibits in a unique fashion. He artistically recontextualized "bits and pieces" culled from scores of sources, the result being assemblages that intrigued and stimulated his audiences. In Florencio's holiday yards folk art genres crossed, interacted and at the same time were interdependent. For example, the *nacimiento* was the setting for *Las Posadas* where participants played and sang traditional music, served traditional food, and played traditional games. For Halloween, characters that looked "modern" and "American" served as a point of departure for storytelling. The assemblage also reminded the viewers of the importance of the Day of the Dead. Florencio created an intricate, colorful, and complex cultural mosaic by layering and combining disparate symbols to encompass his aesthetic. The visual language encoded in Florencio's festive yard displays communicated cultural, family, religious and individual values.

The act of decorating the yard and the connected series of social performances enabled Florencio to illustrate contemporary dilemmas and begin to resolve them. By drawing upon a vast and rich cultural repertoire he used old forms in new ways to express himself, and in so doing, made himself visible in a dramatic way that could not be ignored or forgotten. By creating unique rituals, exemplified by Halloween night or the Mass of December 12, Florencio established his identity in the world, instead of allowing the world to define him. Carolina Morales pointed out that "he wanted people to notice him, he wanted to excel, to not be just anyone, but to be talked about. He wanted people to realize that he had an imagination and a lot of creativity." The way he shared his prolific inventiveness, both inside and outside his community, inspired many others. His yards supplied a haven where strangers and friends could interact, where they were allowed to laugh, cry, reflect, converse and play. Just as Jesus and Mary found shelter in the stable in Bethlehem, Florencio offered us *posada* in the context of his yard.

Aftermath

In preparing for death, Florencio took his family back to his home in Mexico in July 1992. After a two-year debilitating illness, he died there in October 1992 at the age of forty-three. On Halloween and during the Christmas season that year, many people went to his house on Griffin Avenue expecting to see his displays, but the yard was empty. Florencio had told few people of his illness, and many acquaintances did not know that he had died. Those aware of his impending death acknowledged their love and appreciation to him.

A local street artist, Peter Quezada, painted a mural in honor of Florencio (plate 40). Quezada's act illustrated the impact that Florencio, both as artist and citizen, had upon his community. The piece occupies a garage door west of Griffin Avenue on Avenue 43, just around the corner from the Moraleses' home. The mural commands attention from passersby because of its size alone, but it also appears intimate, framed by the architectural structure of the garage and iron railing above it. It depicts a kneeling Christ as a shepherd with head bowed, and a lion and a lamb. The lion and Christ shed tears. A large arching red ribbon inscribed *"dedicado a Florencio Morales, con mucho cariño y amor"* ("dedicated to Florencio Morales with much affection and love") encompasses the central figures. White doves in flight flank the upper corners of the garage door as the other decorative elements—a richly plumed peacock and vine-covered cane—frame the main composition.

Quezada, a prolific streetscaper, knew Florencio and decided to paint a mural for him after he learned of his terminal illness. Although he had only met the man in 1989, he had known of the yard displays since the early 1980s. "The local Northeast Paper would run pictures of his house, and it became, naturally, a Northeast L. A. symbol," said Quezada. "When he used to put his decorations on his house, I didn't know him, but I knew that the person who did this was somebody special because of what he was doing and the flavor that he did it with. I thought, 'You know what? This guy's a nut, but he's a good nut.' You know, people think I'm a nut for doing what it is that I do, which is running around with graffiti writers and with gang members and painting on the walls. They think I'm a nut. But you can be a nut and still be a good person, you know. So I thought, 'This guy's a nut, but he's a good nut,' and when the time came that I met Florencio he was everything that I imagined he would be. He was a very innocent man, he was a very, I don't know, you could use the word sweet. He was a very sweet man."

Quezada and Florencio shared similar visions. Both artists sought to improve their neighborhoods and channel negative energy into something productive. Quezada described how he felt akin to Florencio: "When I met him it wasn't like, 'You're the great Florencio,' or 'You're the Florencio . . .' It was something like, 'Hey, how are you?' It was something natural. And that's the thing about him that's the easiest to describe. He was just natural—easiest thing in the world. That's why for me to do the thing I did for him, it was nothing. And no, I don't do murals for everybody that dies, you know, Jesus Christ, I'd be doing murals for all my buddies, and I've lost a tremendous amount of gang-related friends."

After seeing Florencio in the last stages of his illness, Quezada decided to paint the mural. "When I saw him in March of '92, I said, 'This isn't just an illness. Florencio has the look of a man who has X number of days, to weeks, to months, to live.' And then I said to myself, 'Jesus, I've got to do something for Florencio because he's going to go away.'" Soon after, Quezada began work on the mural with the help of some neighborhood youth. His mission was to complete the work so that Florencio could see it before he died.

When the artists finished the mural in April 1992, Florencio saw it and was deeply moved, almost to the point of tears. But at the same time it excited him. Quezada remembered that Florencio—weakened and dependent on an I.V.—got up, removed his intravenous apparatus, and started brainstorming for *another* mural he wanted Quezada to paint. "He wanted kids up there, he wanted just a lot of religious depictions up there, you know, the standard Virgin Marys, Jesus Christ, and he wanted kids at play. And he wanted to show some of the stuff that he had on display." Florencio's desire to inspire another mural showed his depth of passion for creative expression. As a man on his deathbed, he was still elaborating on his vision for the community.

References

Arora, Shirley L. 1981. "La Llorona: The Naturalization of a Legend." *Southwest Folklore* 5 (1):23-40.

Babcock, Barbara. 1978. "Introduction." In *The Reversible World: Symbolic Inversion in Art and Society,* ed. Barbara Babcock, 13-36. Ithaca and London: Cornell University Press.

Boyer, Edward J. 1988. "Holidays Bring Out His Urge to Create Spectacular Yard Displays." *Los Angeles Times,* 11/24. Metro, p. 1, pt. 2, col. 3.

Bronner, Simon J. 1983. "Links to Behavior: An Analysis of Chain Carving." *Kentucky Folklore Record* 29:72-82.

Cadaval, Olivia. 1985. "'The Taking of the Renwick': The Celebration of the Day of the Dead and the Latino Community in Washington, D.C." *Journal of Folklore Research* 22:179-93.

Carmichael, Elizabeth and Chloë Sayer. 1991. *The Skeleton at the Feast: The Day of the Dead in Mexico.* London and Austin, Texas: The British Museum and University of Texas Press.

Día de los Muertos. 1990. Mexican Fine Arts Center Museum, Chicago.

Día de los Muertos: An Exhibition Based on the Mexican and Central American Annual Tradition Celebrating and Honoring the Dead. 1988. Alternative Museum, New York City, Nov. 2-Dec. 23.

Dorman, Artell. 1959. "Speak of the Devil." In *And Horns on the Toads,* eds. Mody C. Boatright, Wilson M. Hudson and Allen Maxwell, 142-46. Dallas, Texas: Southern Methodist University Press.

Griffith, James S. 1987. "Baroque Principles of Organization in Contemporary Mexican American Arizona." Unpublished paper presented at American Folklore Society annual meeting, Albuquerque.

______. 1988. "Posadas, Nacimientos and Tamales." *Tucson Guide Quarterly.* Dec. 1988:72-74, 117-22.

Heisley, Michael and Mary MacGregor-Villarreal. 1991. *More Than a Tradition: Mexican-American Nacimientos in Los Angeles.* Los Angeles: The Southwest Museum.

Jasper, Pat and Kay Turner, eds. 1986. *Art Among Us, Arte Entre Nosotros; Mexican American Folk Art of San Antonio.* San Antonio: San Antonio Museum Association.

Jones, Michael Owen. 1971. "The Concept of Aesthetic in the Traditional Arts." *Western Folklore* 30(2):77-104.

______. 1989. *Craftsman of the Cumberlands: Tradition and Creativity.* Lexington: The University Press of Kentucky.

Jones, Pamela. 1988. "'There Was a Woman': La Llorona in Oregon." *Western Folklore* 47:195-211.

La Muerte: Expresiones Mexicanas de un Enigma. 1974. Museo Universitario, Universidad Nacional Autónoma de México. Dirección General de Difusión Cultural. Noviembre de 1974/ Abril de 1975.

Los Angeles Times. 1989. "Gardener Raises Bumper Crop of Ghouls." 10/31/89, Home Edition, Metro, p. 3, pt. B, col. 1.

MacGregor-Villarreal, Mary. 1980. "Celebrating Las Posadas in Los Angeles." *Western Folklore* 39:71-105.

Melville, Margarita. 1978. "The Mexican-American and the Celebration of the Fiestas Patrias: An Ethnohistorical Analysis." *Grito del Sol* 3 (Jan-Mar.):107-16.

Myerhoff, Barbara. 1977. "We Don't Wrap Herring in a Printed Page: Fusion, Fictions and Continuity in Secular Ritual." In *Secular Ritual*, eds. Sally F. Moore and Barbara G. Myerhoff, 199-217. Amsterdam: Van Gorcum.

Paredes, Américo. 1970. *Folktales of Mexico*. Chicago: University of Chicago Press.

Robe, Stanley. 1971. *Mexican Tales and Legends from Veracruz*. Berkeley: University of California Press.

Santino, Jack. 1986. "The Folk Assemblage of Autumn: Tradition and Creativity in Halloween Art." In *Folk Art and Art Worlds*, eds. John Michael Vlach and Simon J. Bronner, 151-69. Ann Arbor: UMI Research Press.

Seriff, Suzanne and José Limón. 1986. "Bits and Pieces: The Mexican American Folk Aesthetic." In *Art Among Us, Arte Entre Nosotros; Mexican American Folk Art of San Antonio*, eds. Pat Jasper and Kay Turner, 40-49. San Antonio: San Antonio Museum Association.

Sheehy, Colleen. 1991. "The Flamingo in the Garden: Artifice, Aesthetics, and Popular Taste in American Yard Art." Ph. D. dissertation, American Studies, University of Minnesota.

Sommers, Laurie Kay. 1985. "Symbol and Style in Cinco de Mayo." *Journal of American Folklore* 98:476-82.

Stern, Stephen. 1991. "Introduction." In *Creative Ethnicity: Symbols and Strategies of Contemporary Ethnic Life*, eds. Stephen Stern and John Allan Cicala, xi-xx. Logan: Utah State University Press.

Toor, Frances. 1947. *A Treasury of Mexican Folkways*. New York: Crown Publishers.

Turner, Kay. 1982. "Mexican American Home Altars: Towards Their Interpretation." *Aztlan* 13-14:309-26.

Turner, Victor. 1974. "Hidalgo: History as Social Drama." In *Dramas, Fields and Metaphors: Symbolic Action in Human Society*, 98-155. Ithaca: Cornell University Press.

Wallrich, William Jones. 1950. "Some Variants of the 'Demon Dancer.'" *Western Folklore* 9:144-46.

Wolf, Eric R. 1958. "The Virgin of Guadalupe: A Mexican National Symbol." *Journal of American Folklore* 71:34-39.

Interviews

The following tape-recorded interviews greatly contributed to my understanding of Florencio Morales's yard art: Peter Quezada 5/31/93; Alberto, Alfonso and Carolina Morales 5/22/93, conducted in Spanish, with translator Alex Todorovic; Paul Jenkins 10/26/90; Cristina Díaz 12/10/89; Florencio Morales 12/7/89, 11/24/89.

In this work, I have also incorporated information from other informal (nonrecorded) interviews and conversations with Florencio Morales, Petri Gonzáles, Edward Boyer, Kitty Vasconcelos, George Rivera, and Juan Esteves.

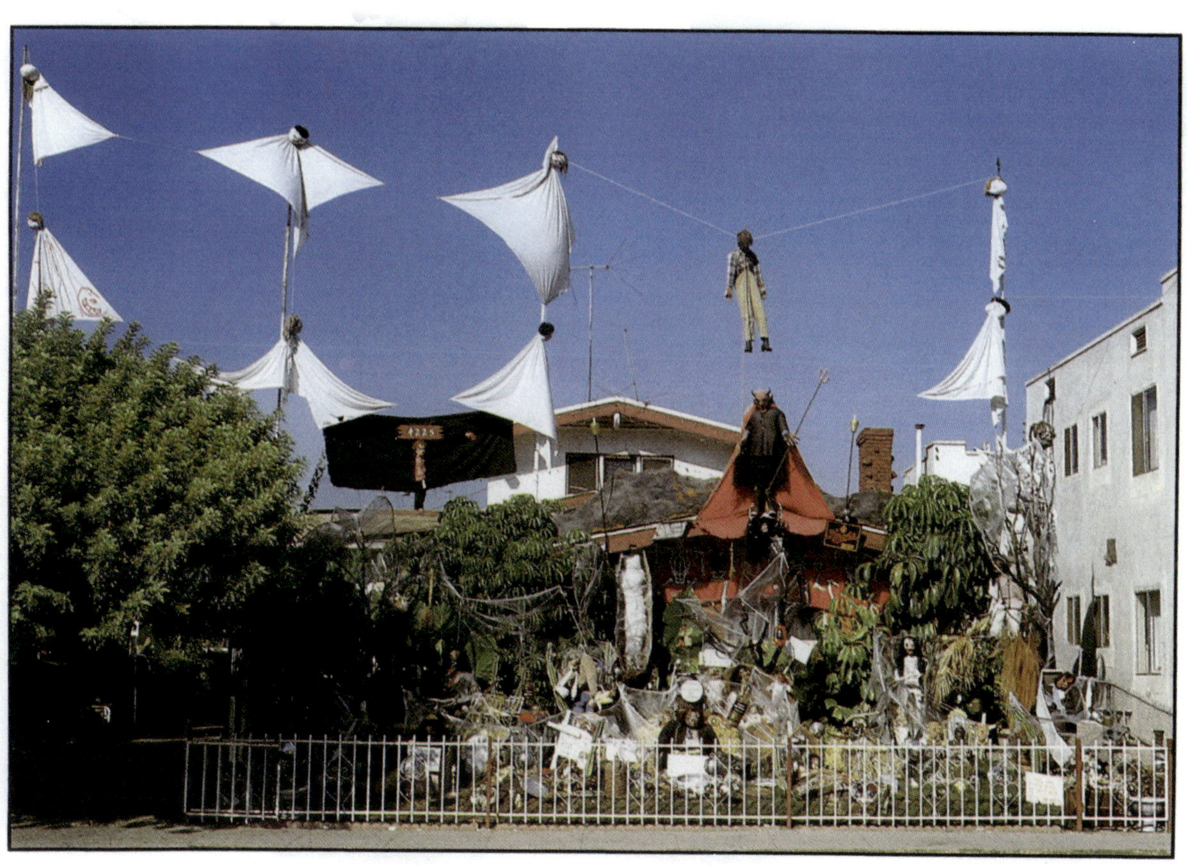

PLATE I
Florencio Morales's 1990 Halloween display at 4225 Griffin Avenue in Los Angeles.

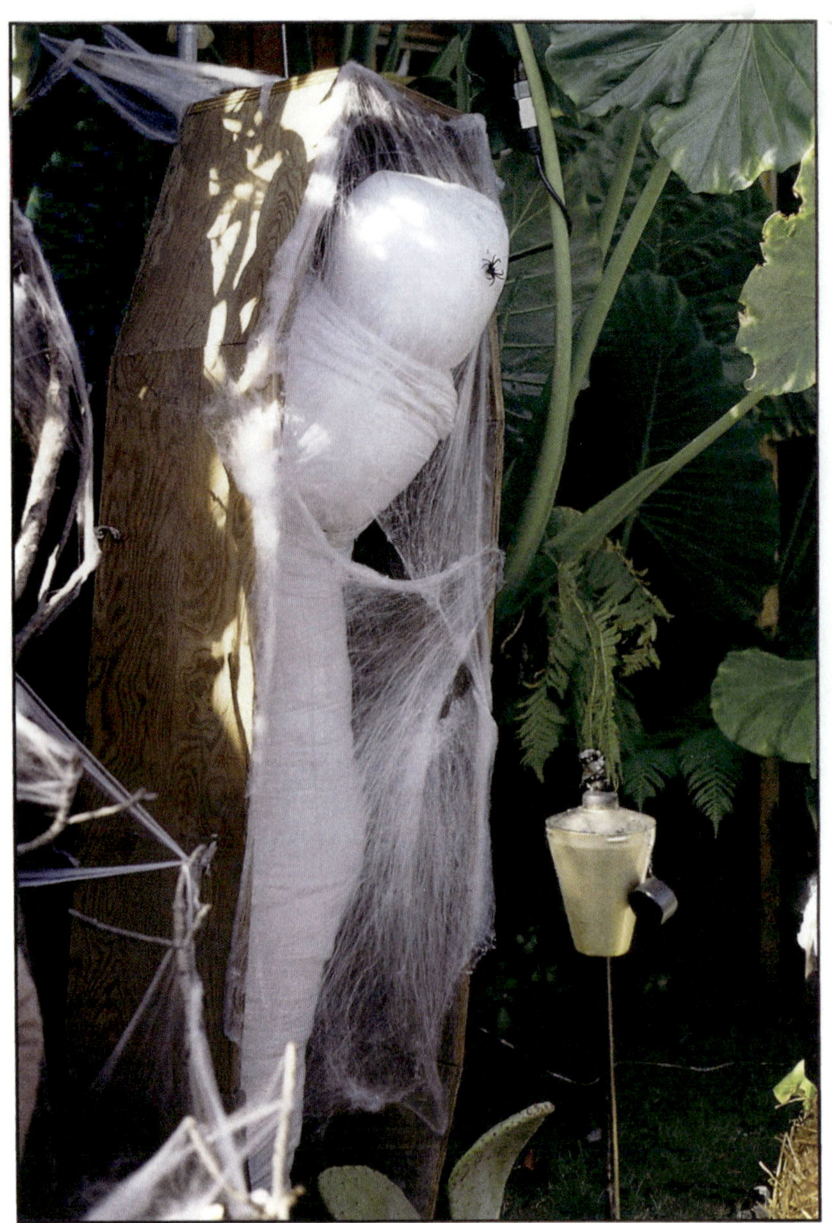

PLATE 2
Handmade mummy and coffin. At right stands a torch for nighttime illumination (Halloween 1989).

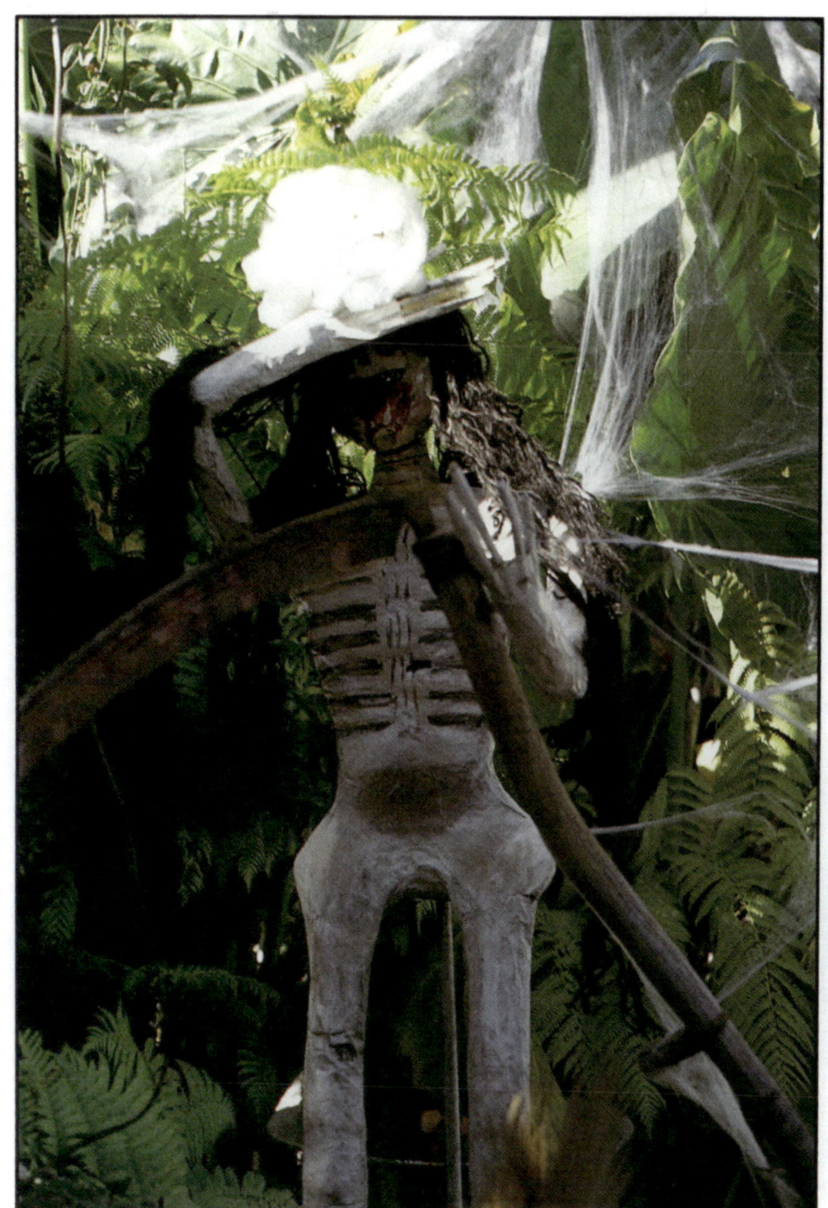

PLATE 3
A life-size papier maché skeleton personifies Death (Halloween 1989).

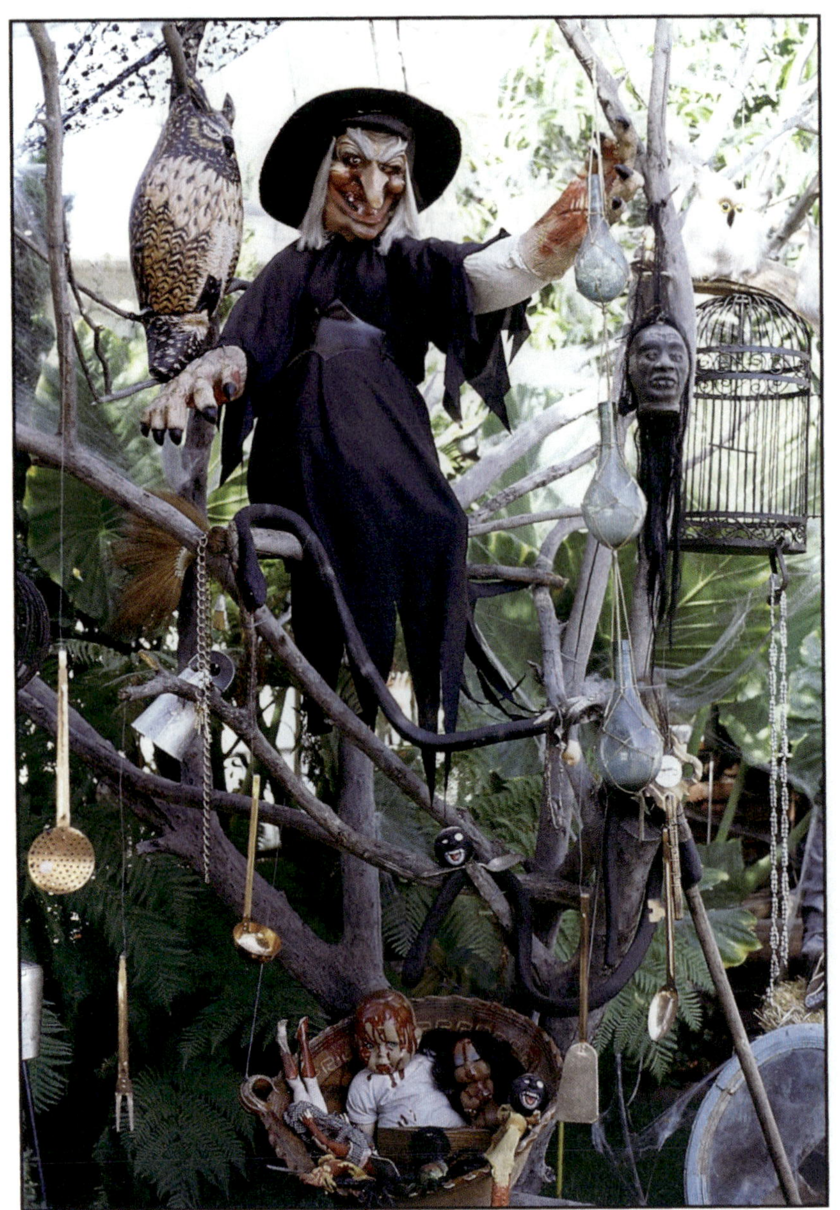

PLATE 4
A legless witch hangs from a dead tree planted for this occasion. She hovers above her cache of bloodied infants and chickens reserved for feasting (Halloween 1990).

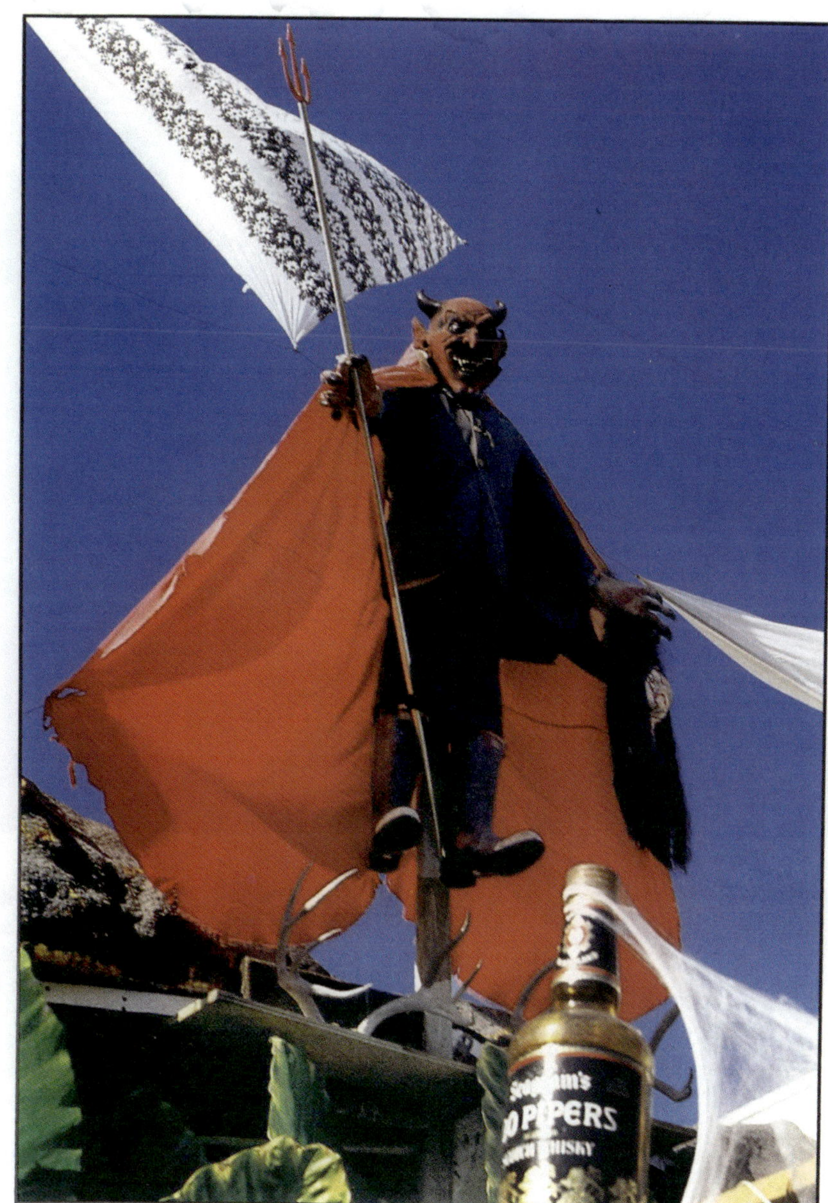

PLATE 5
The figure of Satan reigns on high. He holds the decapitated head of one of his victims (Halloween 1989).

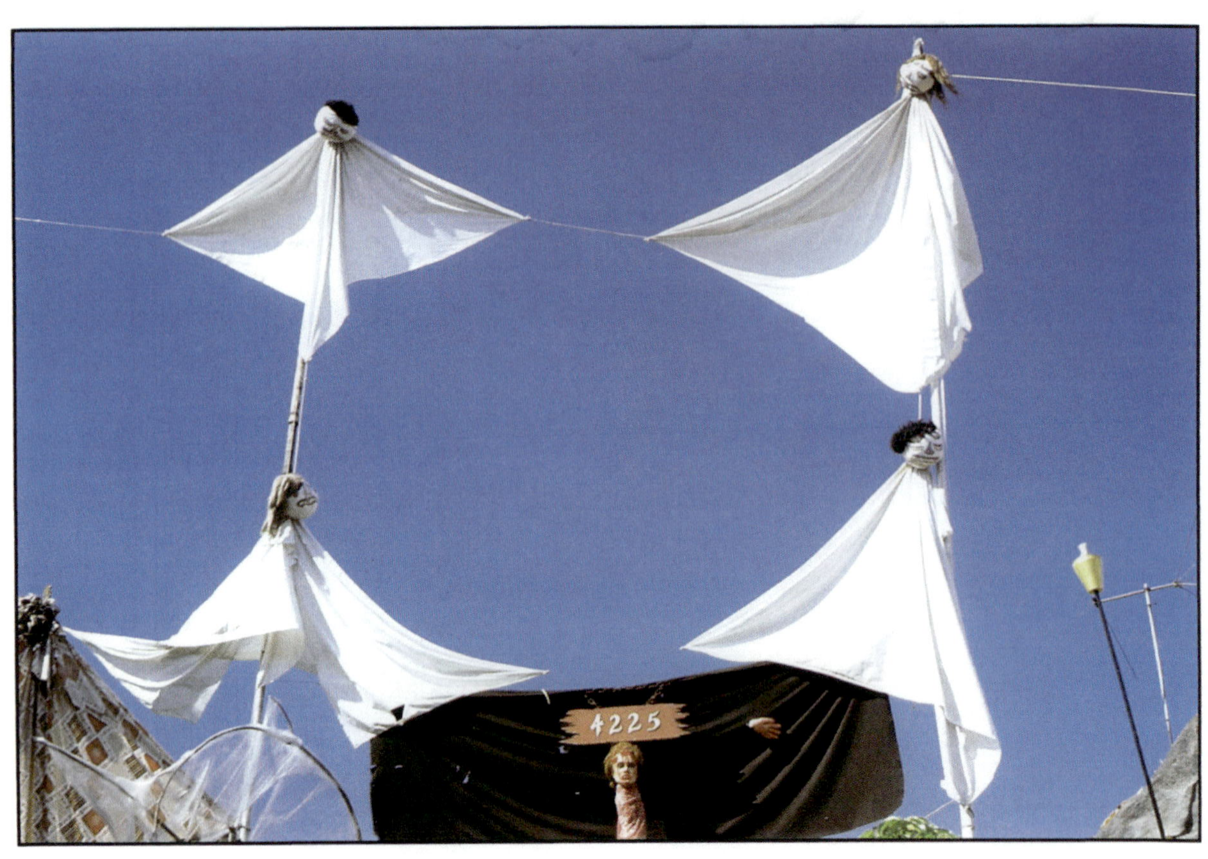

PLATE 6
Wig-wearing ghosts made from sheets billow in the wind above the house. Florencio displays his address prominently by placing a black swath of material behind it supporting a disembodied head and hand (Halloween 1990).

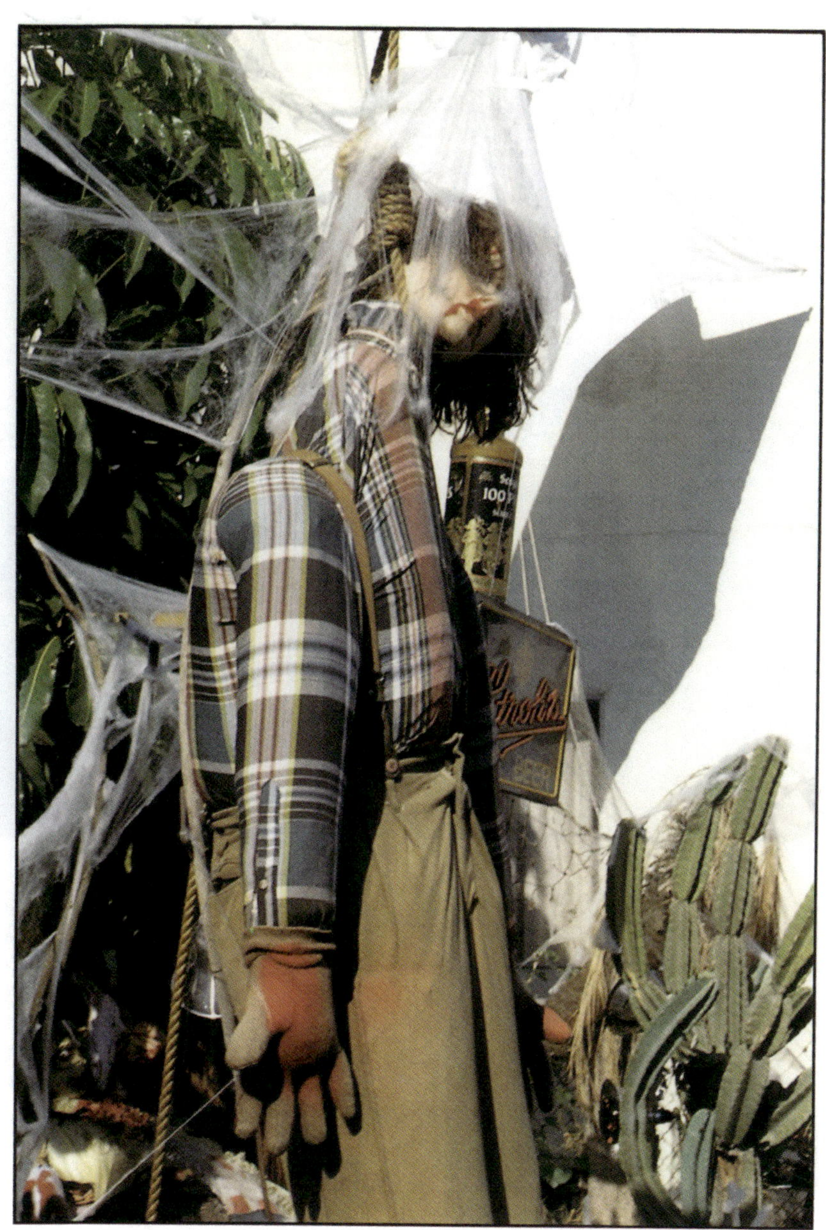

PLATE 7
Cobweb-sheathed victim hangs from a tree (Halloween 1989). This is a version of the original figure Florencio displayed in 1981 that led to the elaborate arrays in following years. Since it represented the genesis of his exhibit, Florencio always placed it in a prominent location. In 1990, he elevated it above the roof in the center.

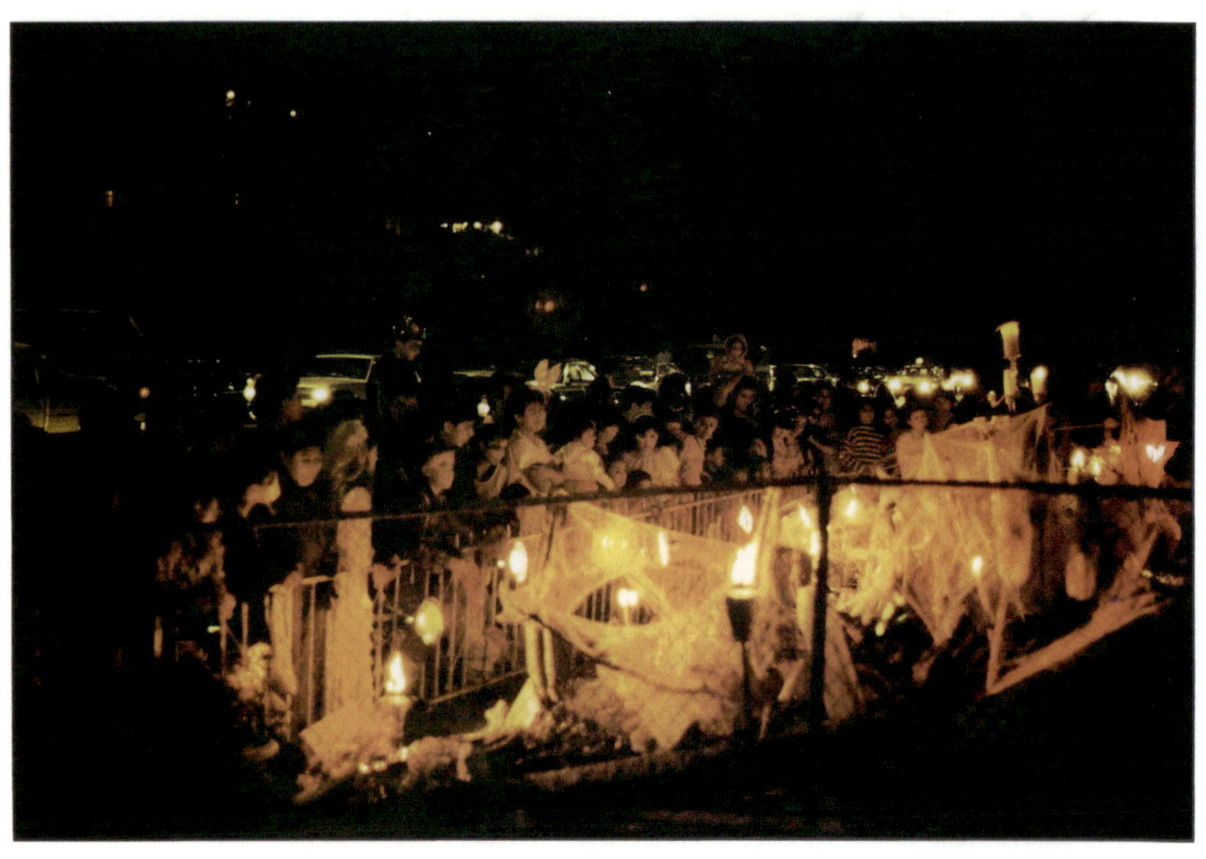

PLATE 8
View from the yard exhibit looking toward the street at party participants filling the sidewalk and the endless stream of cars driving by on Halloween night (1990).

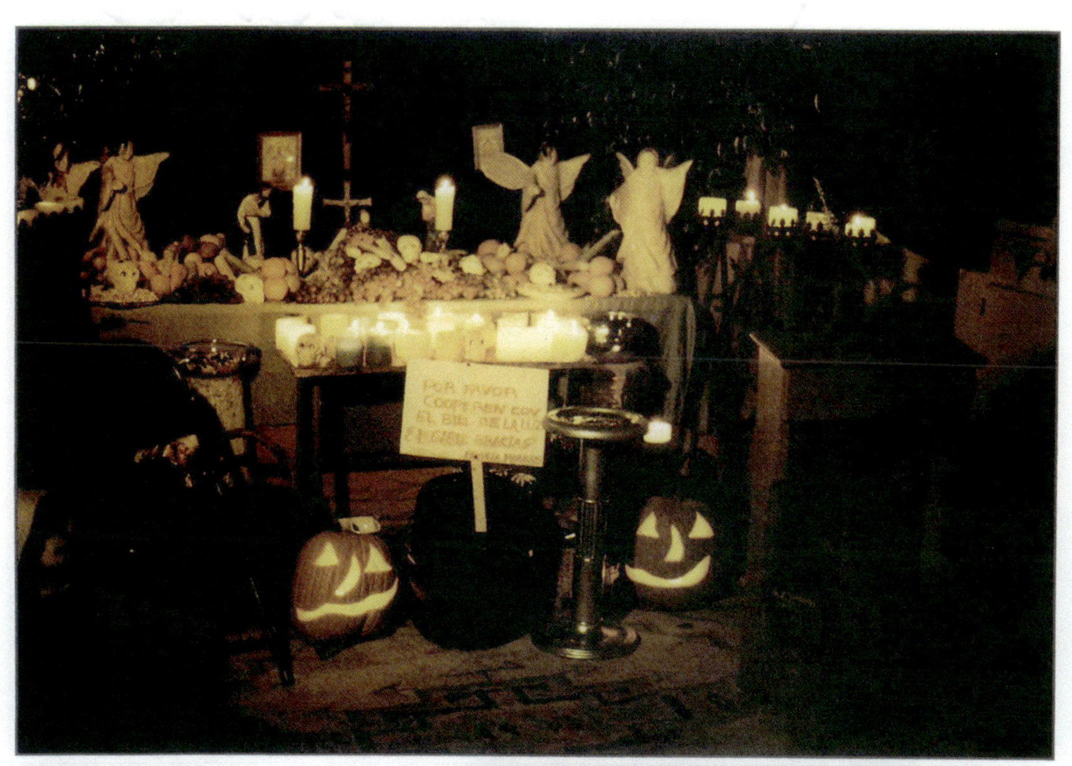

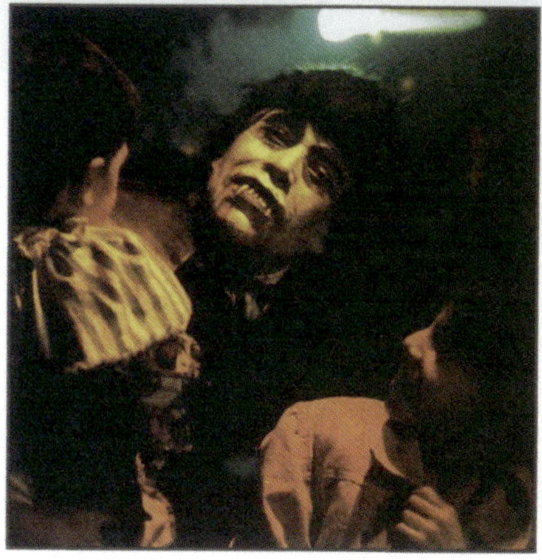

PLATE 9
Altar commemorating *El Día de los Muertos* placed in the driveway adjacent to the yard (Halloween 1990).

PLATE 10
Florencio as Count Dracula on Halloween night (1990).

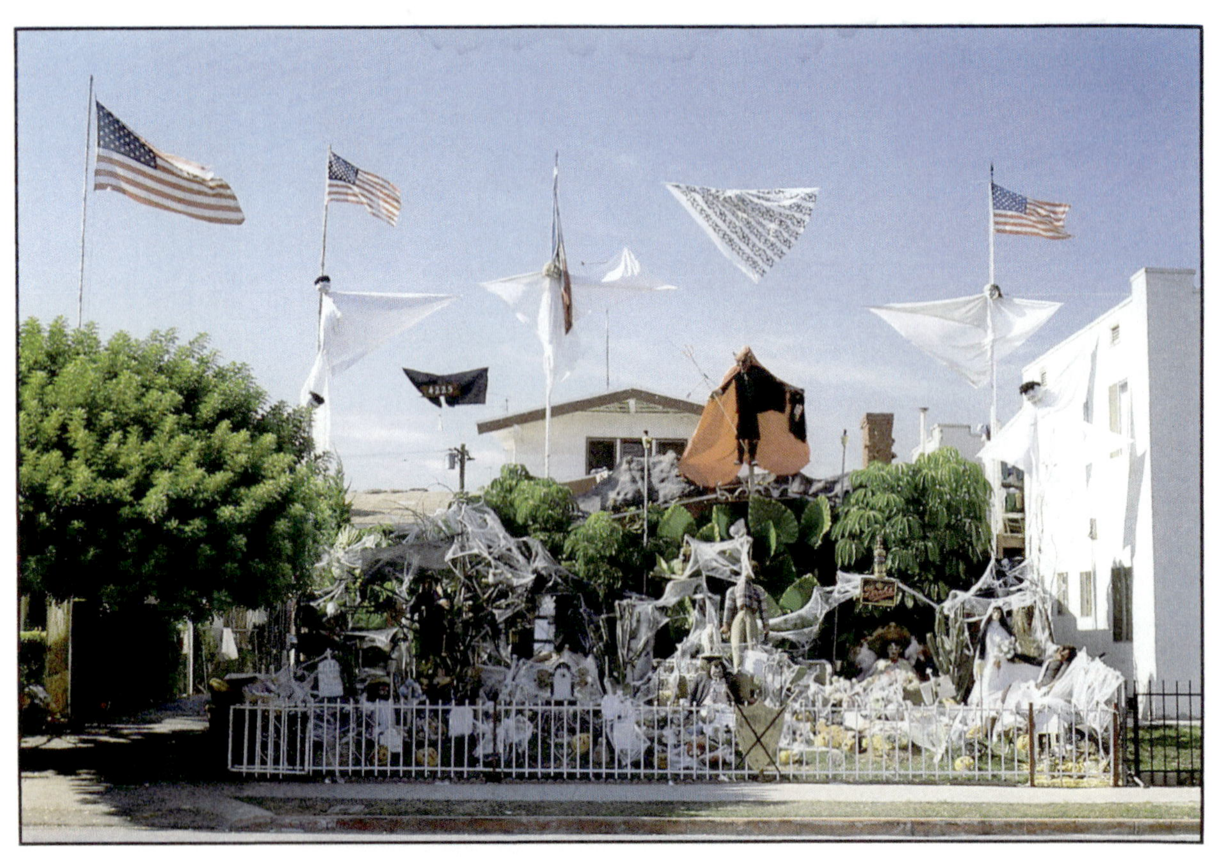

PLATE II
The Halloween display in 1989. This photograph provides a comparison with the 1990 exhibit (Plate I).

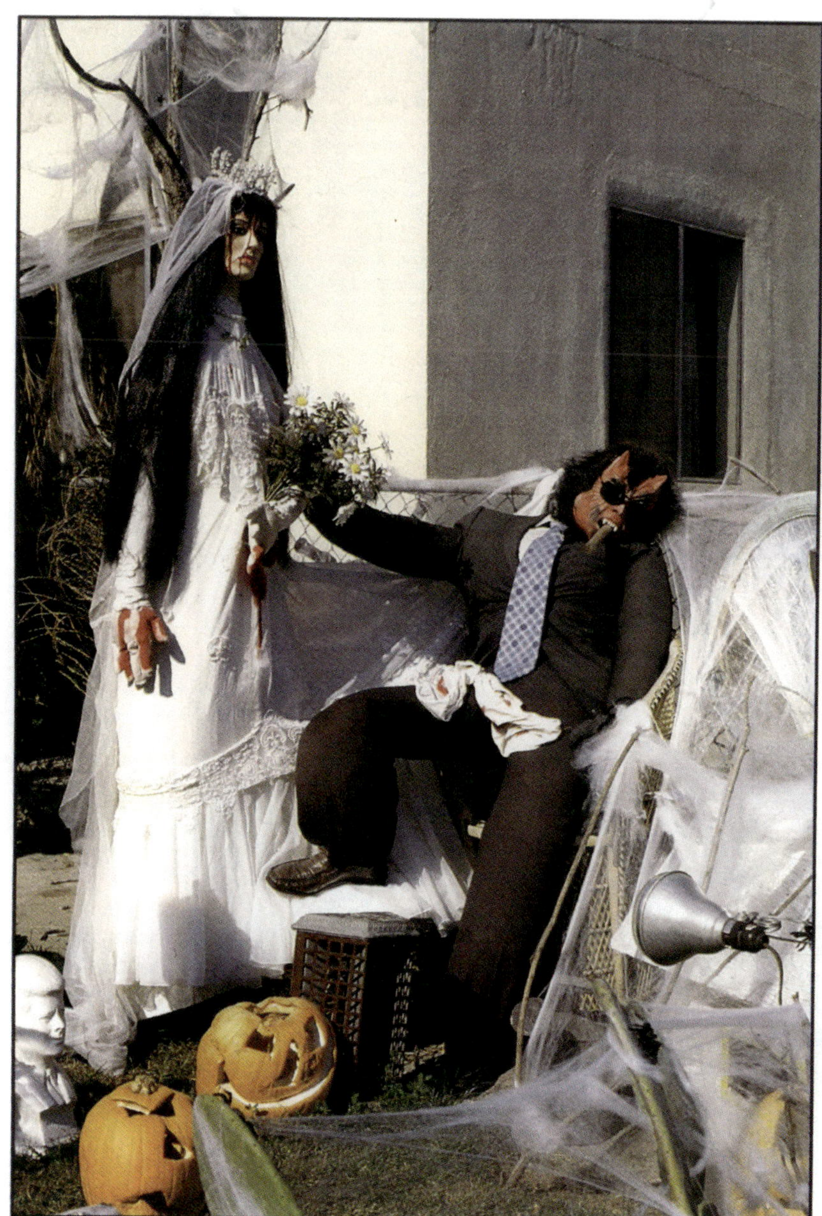

PLATE 12
The devil and his bride pictured here were inspired by the Mexican legend known as "The Demon Dancer" (Halloween 1989).

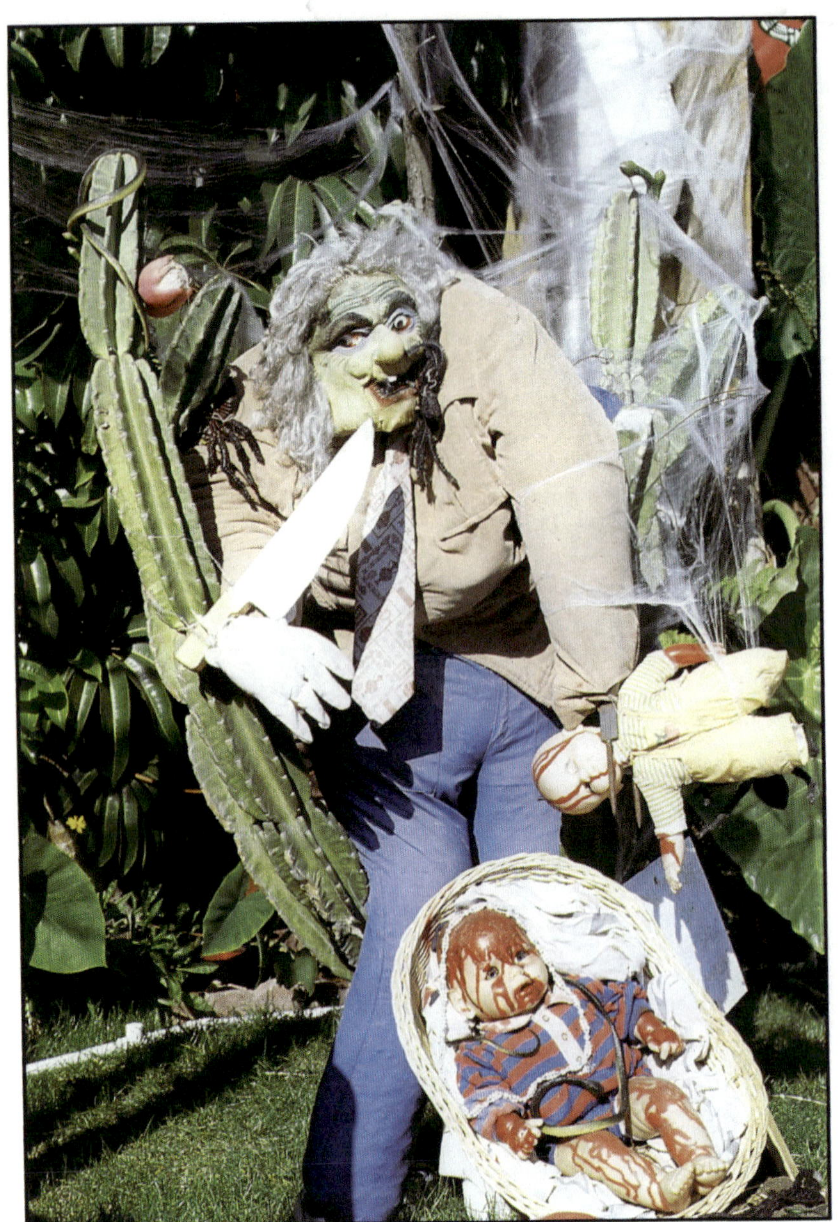

PLATE 13
A grinning baby snatcher holds a bloodied infant by the "hand" (Halloween 1990).

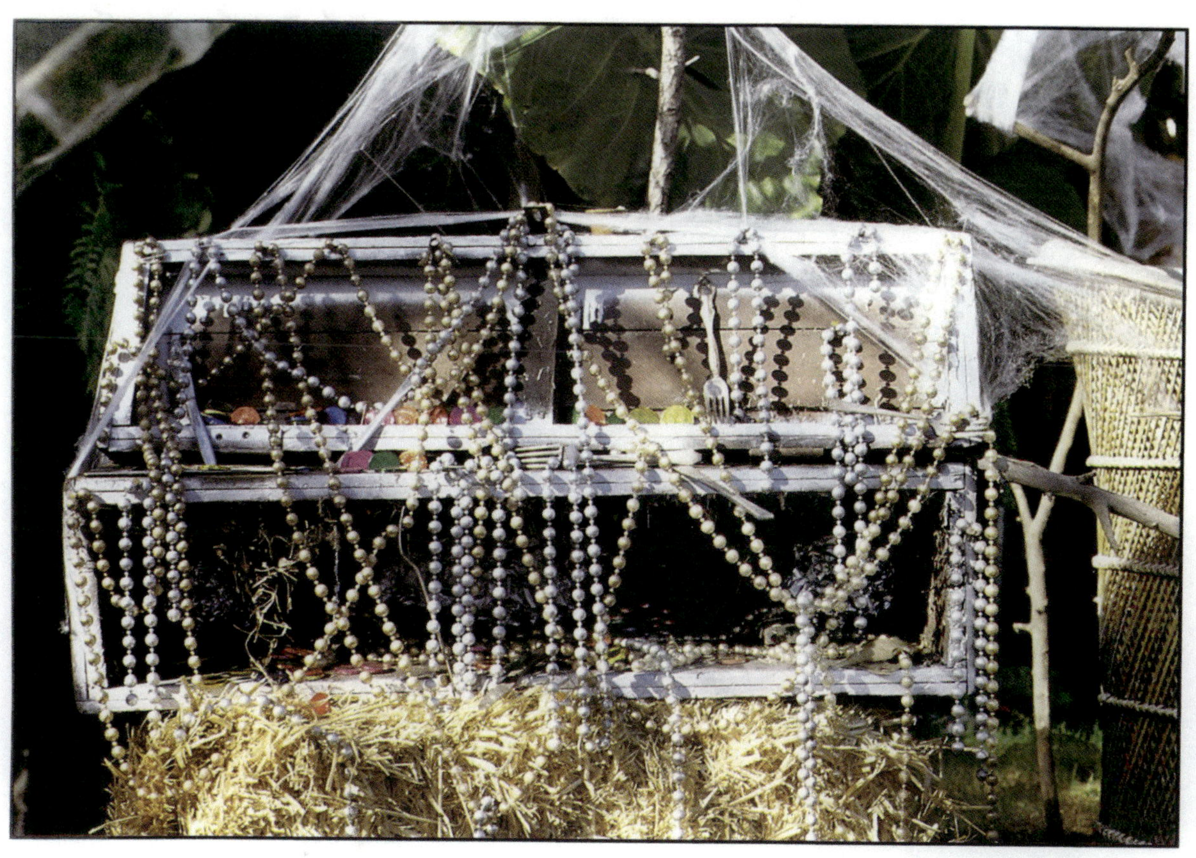

PLATE 14
The elusive treasure chest forecast in Florencio's dream (Halloween 1989).

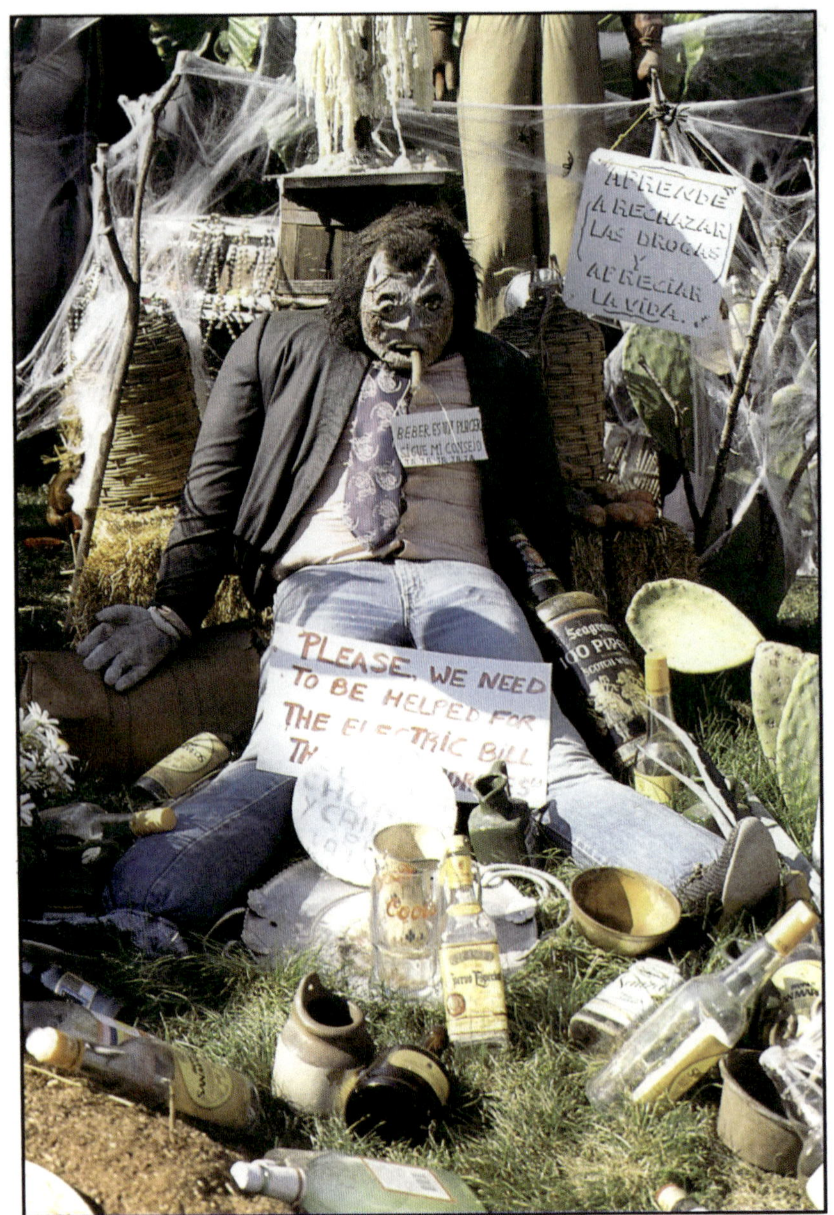

PLATE 15
A cigar-smoking werewolf simultaneously warns of the dangers of alcohol abuse and requests donations for the electric bill (Halloween 1989).

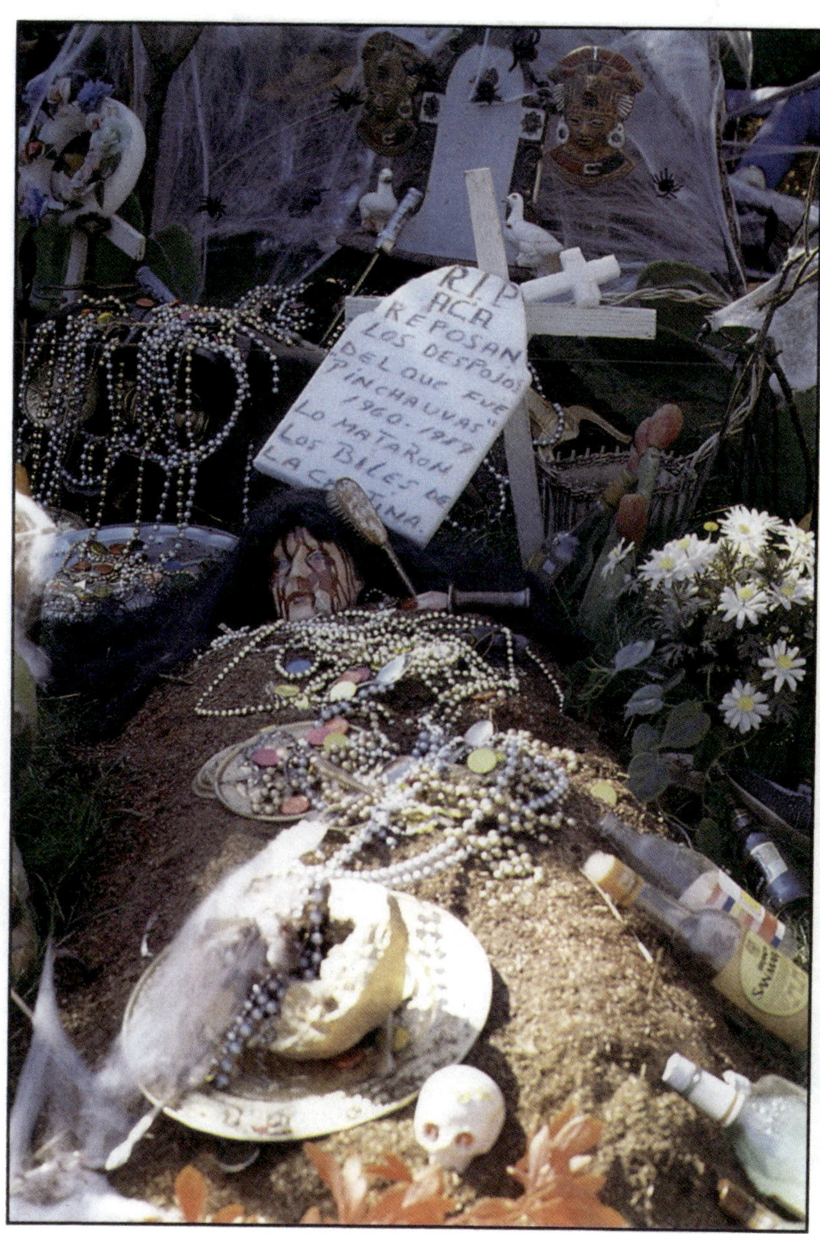

PLATE 16
One of the burial mounds covered with mock *offrendas* (offerings). The epitaph reads, *"R.I.P. Aca reposan los despojos del que fue 'Pinchauvas'—1960-1989—Lo mataron los biles de la cantina"* ("R.I.P. Here lie the remains of "the grape-sucker"—1960-1989—The bar tabs killed him") (Halloween 1989).

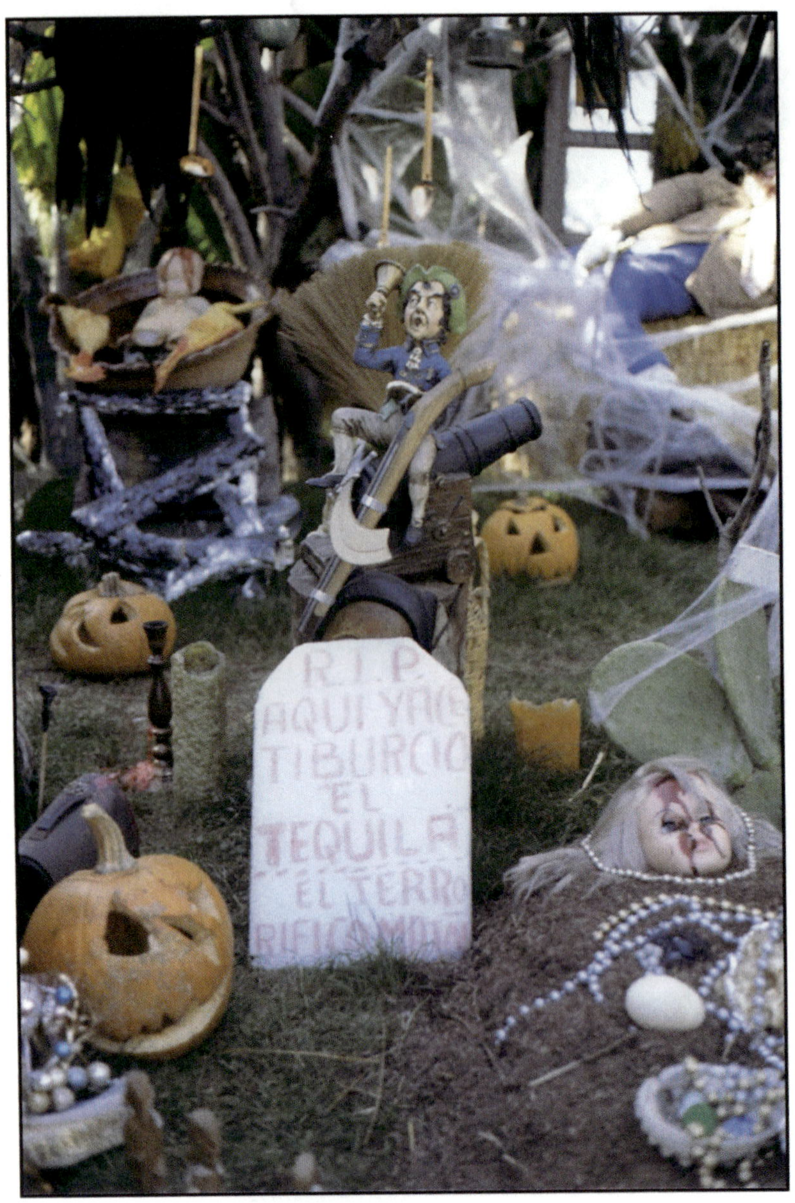

PLATE 17
This statuette of a pirate represents a humorous tribute to Florencio's friend, Tiburcio. The sign declares, *"R.I.P. Aquí yace Tiburcio 'El Tequila,' el terrorífico matón"* ("R.I.P. Here lies Tiburcio Tequila," the terrifying killer") (Halloween 1989).

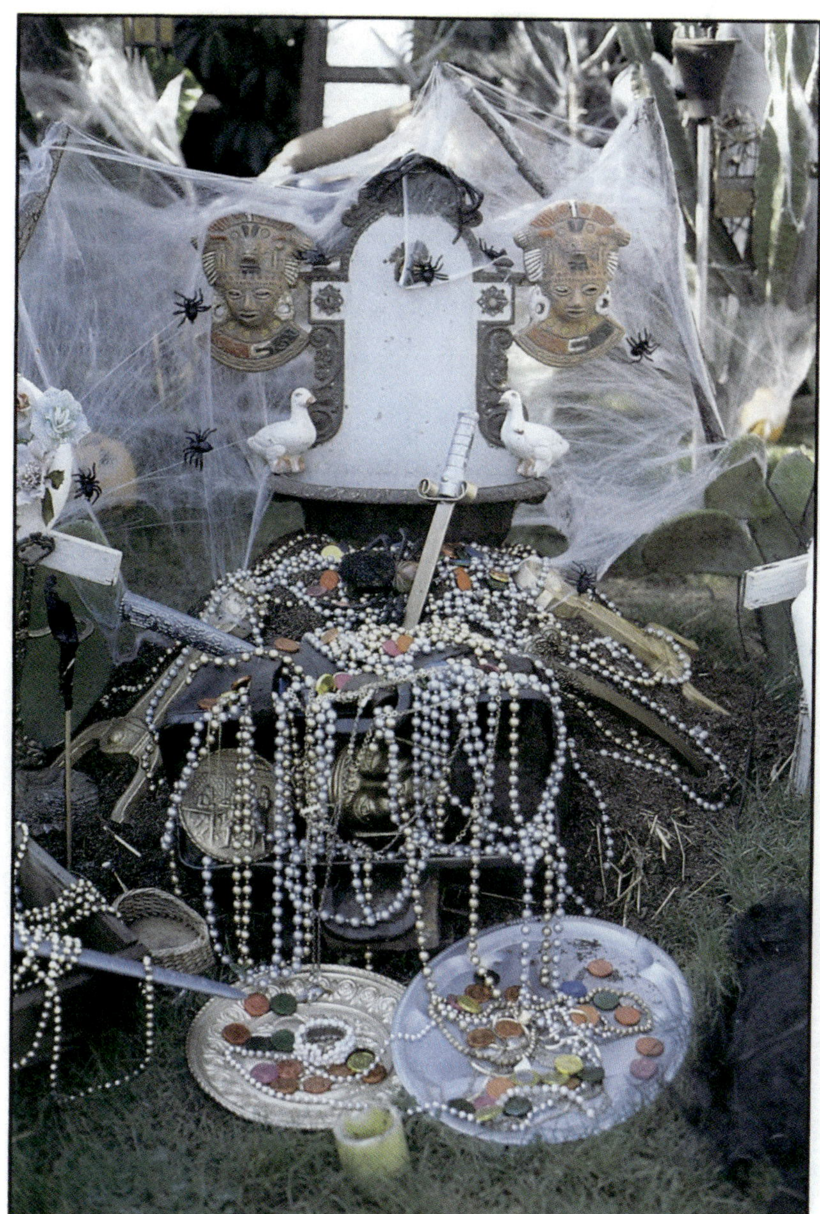

PLATE 18
Aztec tomb representing the results of the Spanish conquest (Halloween 1989).

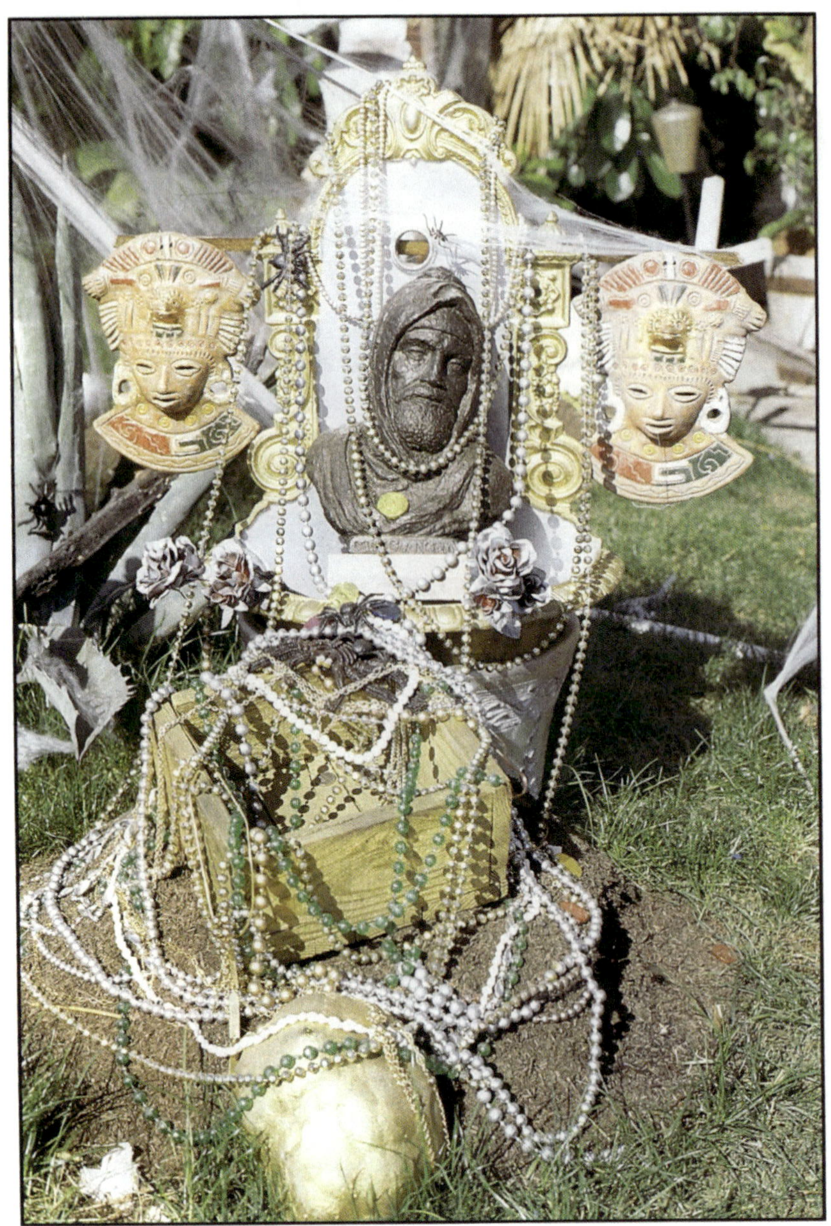

PLATE 19
This 1990 version of the "Aztec tomb" takes on different meanings with the inclusion of the bust of Michelangelo (Halloween 1990).

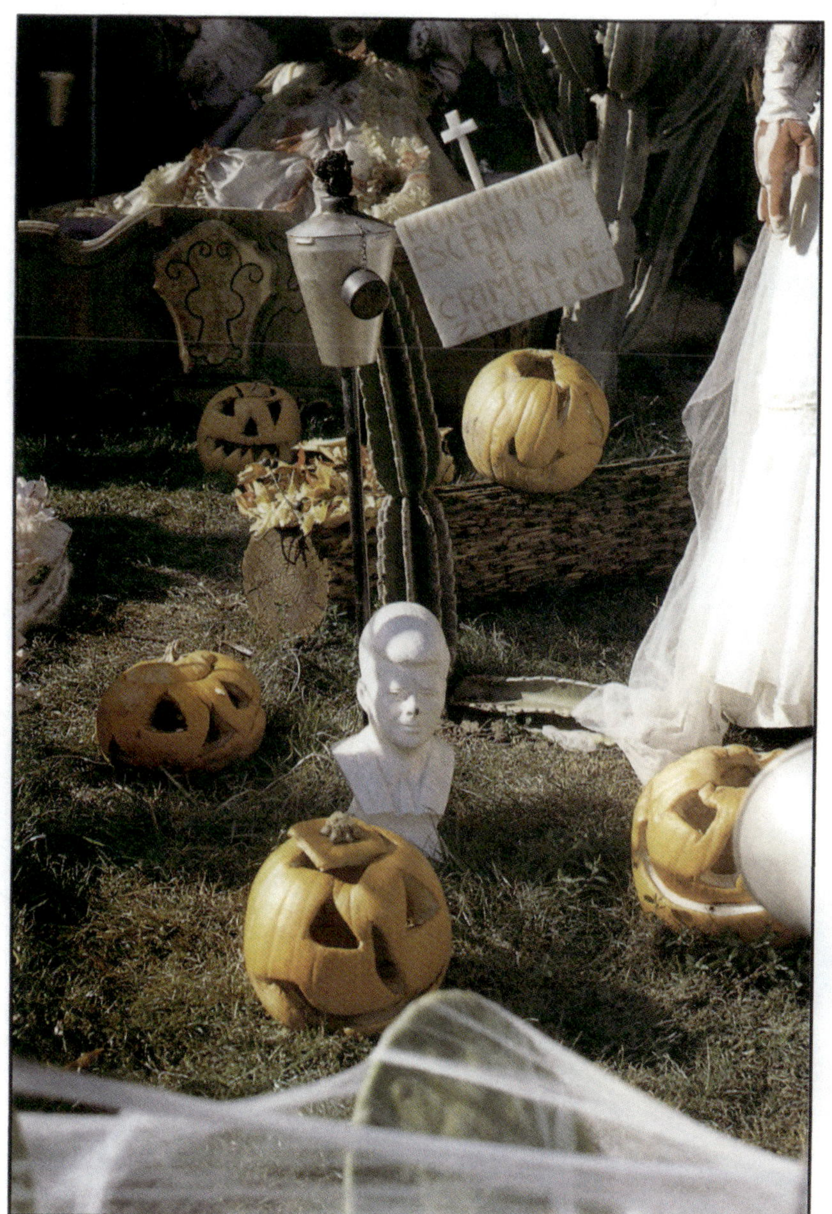

PLATE 20
Bust of John F. Kennedy amid patch of jack-o'-lanterns with torch (Halloween 1989).

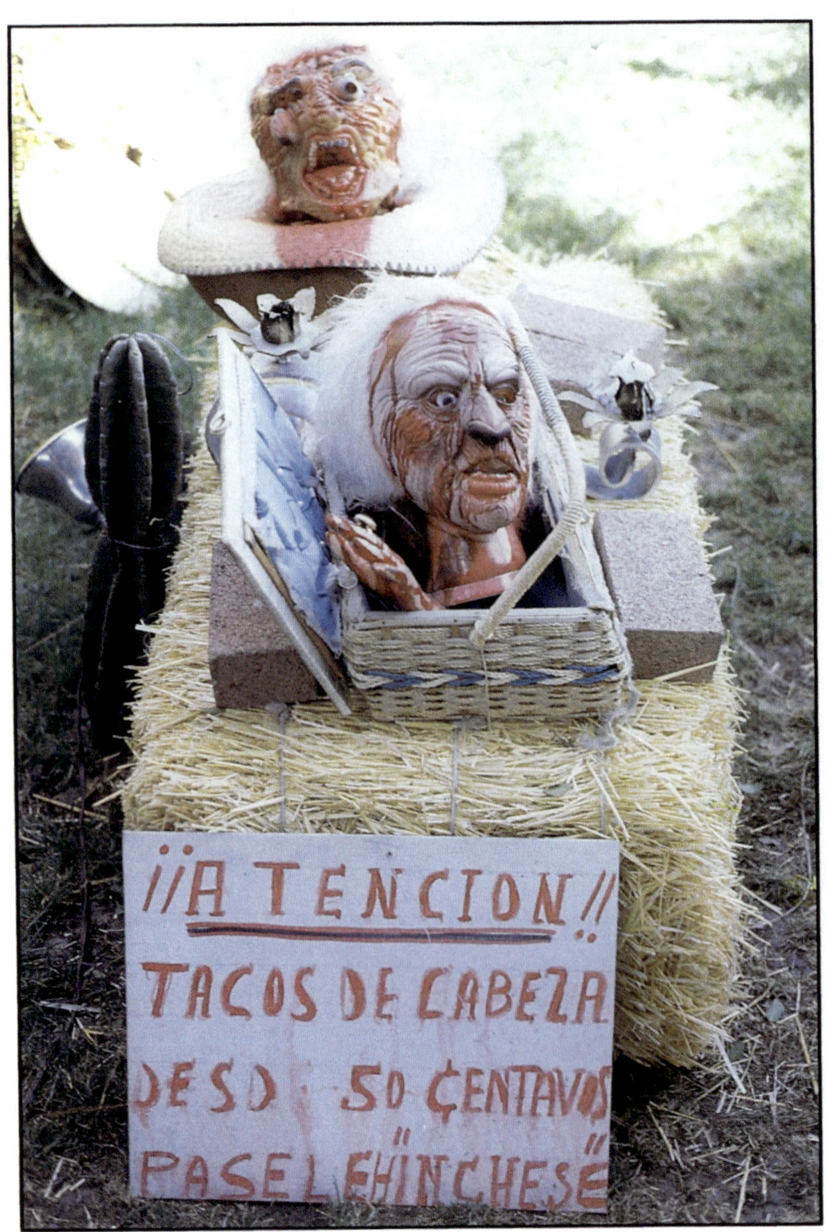

PLATE 21
This horrific scene illustrates a visual pun. The sign reads, "*¡Atención! Tacos de cabeza—50 centavos—Pásele 'hínchese'*" ("Notice! Brain tacos—50 cents—'Dig right in'"). *Tacos de cabeza* actually exist as a culinary delicacy, but the ingredient *cabeza* consists of cow's brains as the filling for taco shells rather than human head meat (Halloween 1990).

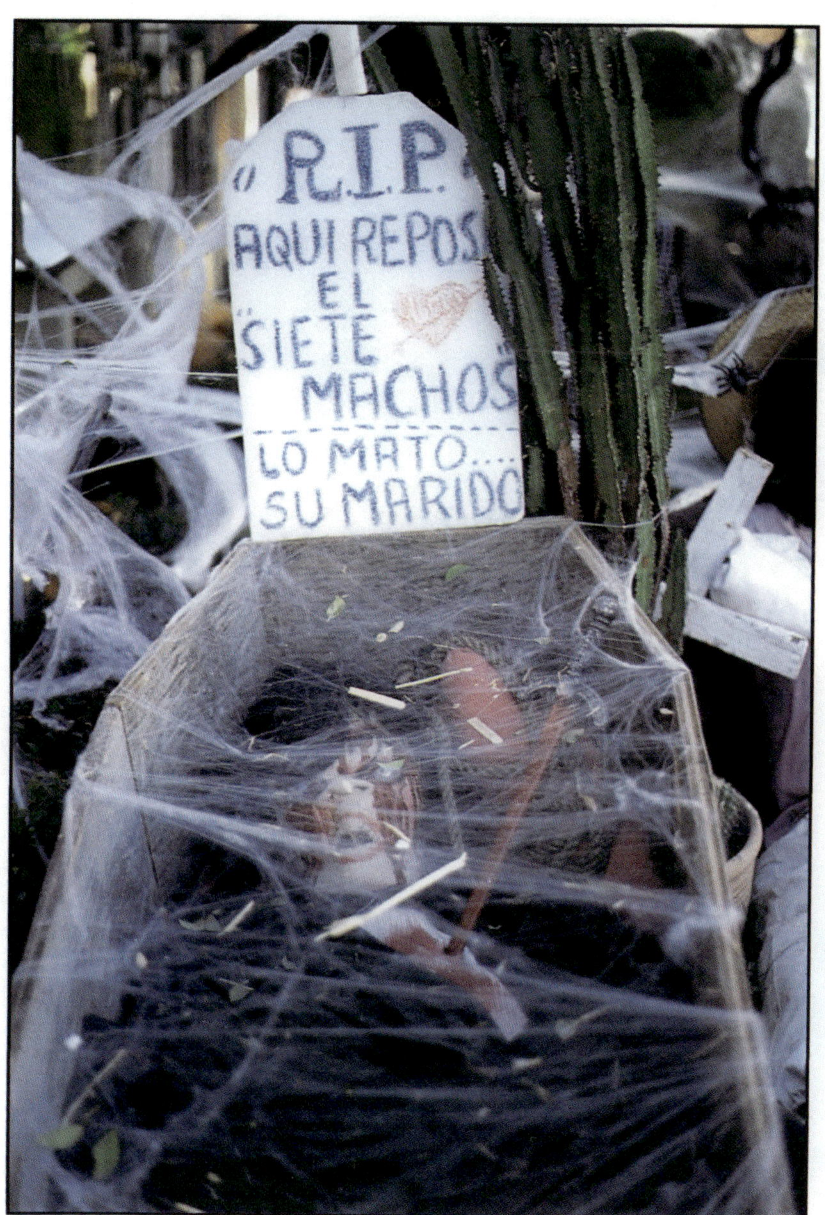

PLATE 22
The epitaph, which reads, *"R.I.P. Aquí reposa El 'Siete Machos,' lo mató... su marido"* ("R.I.P. Here lies the seven times macho, his husband killed him") defines this character as the victim of a complicated love triangle (Halloween 1989).

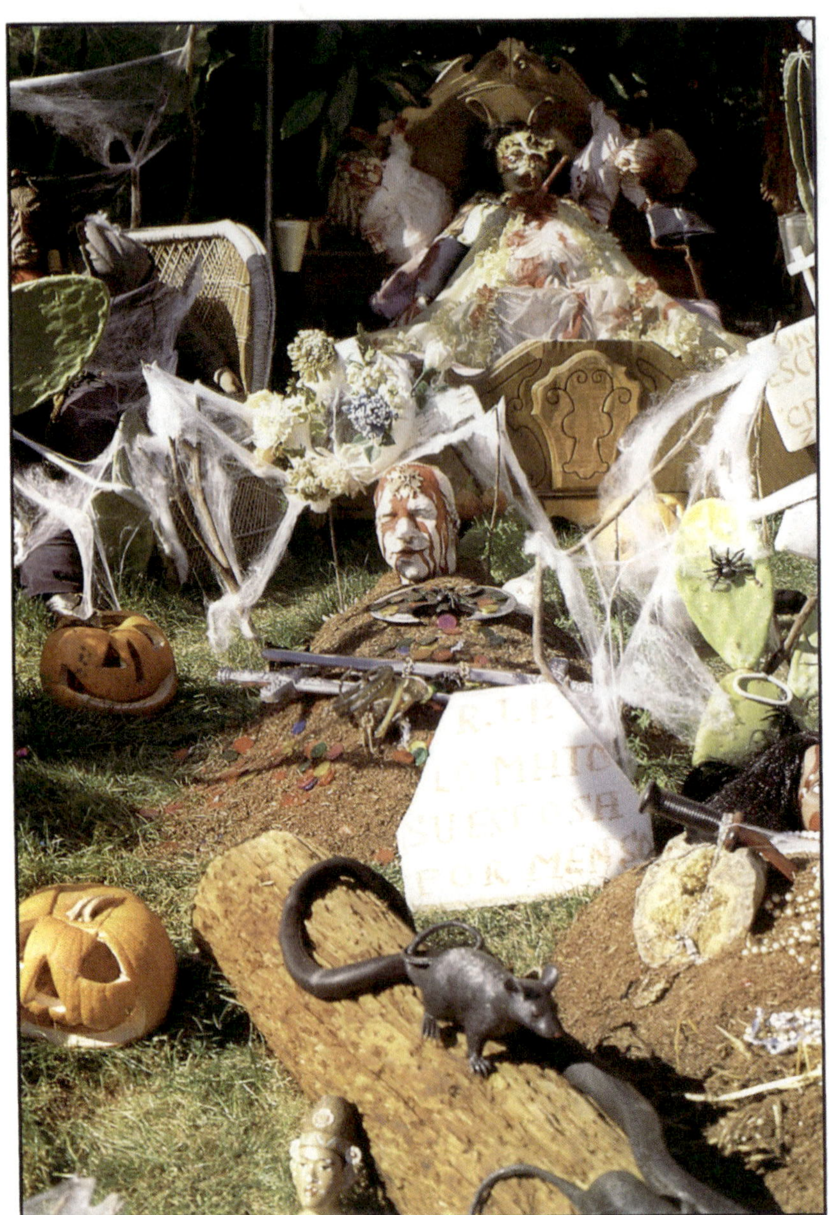

PLATE 23
The stone-faced miser (in center) stares at his wealth piled on top of his burial mound (Halloween 1989).

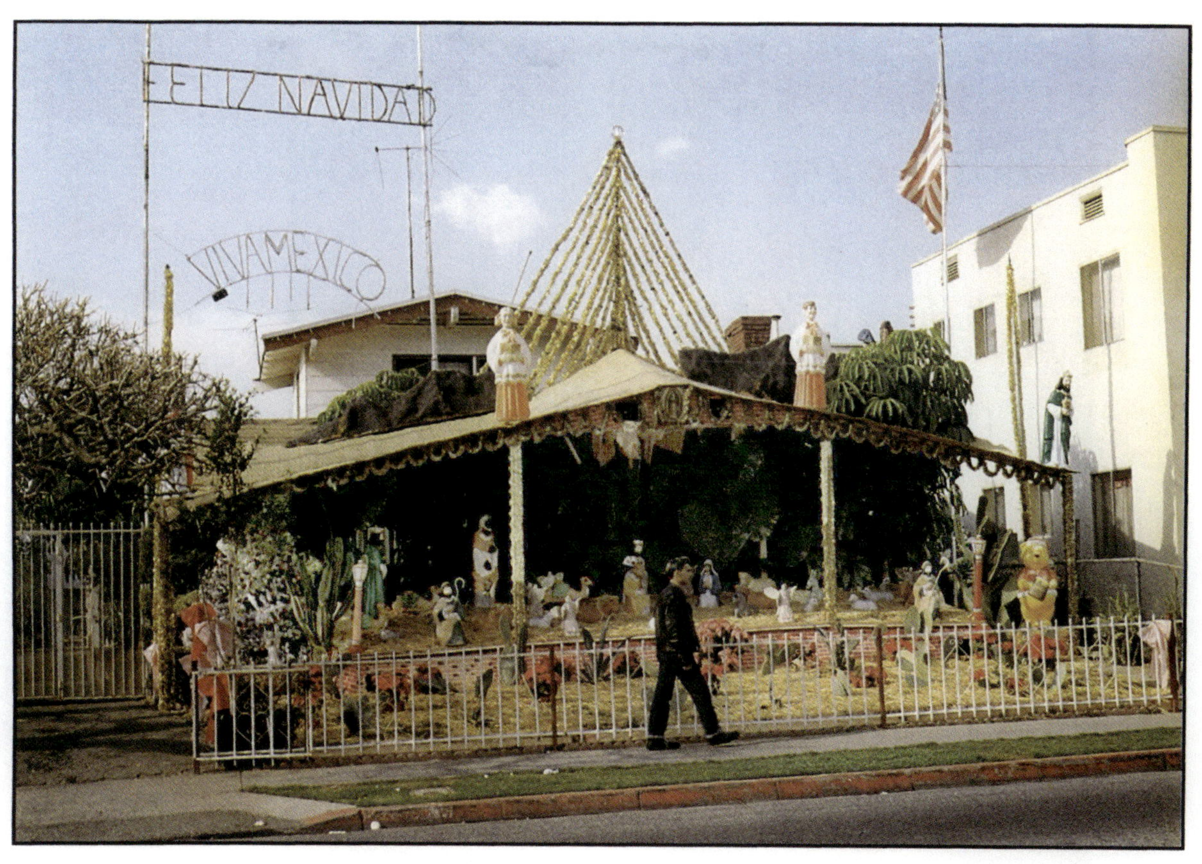

PLATE 24
The Christmas display (1989).

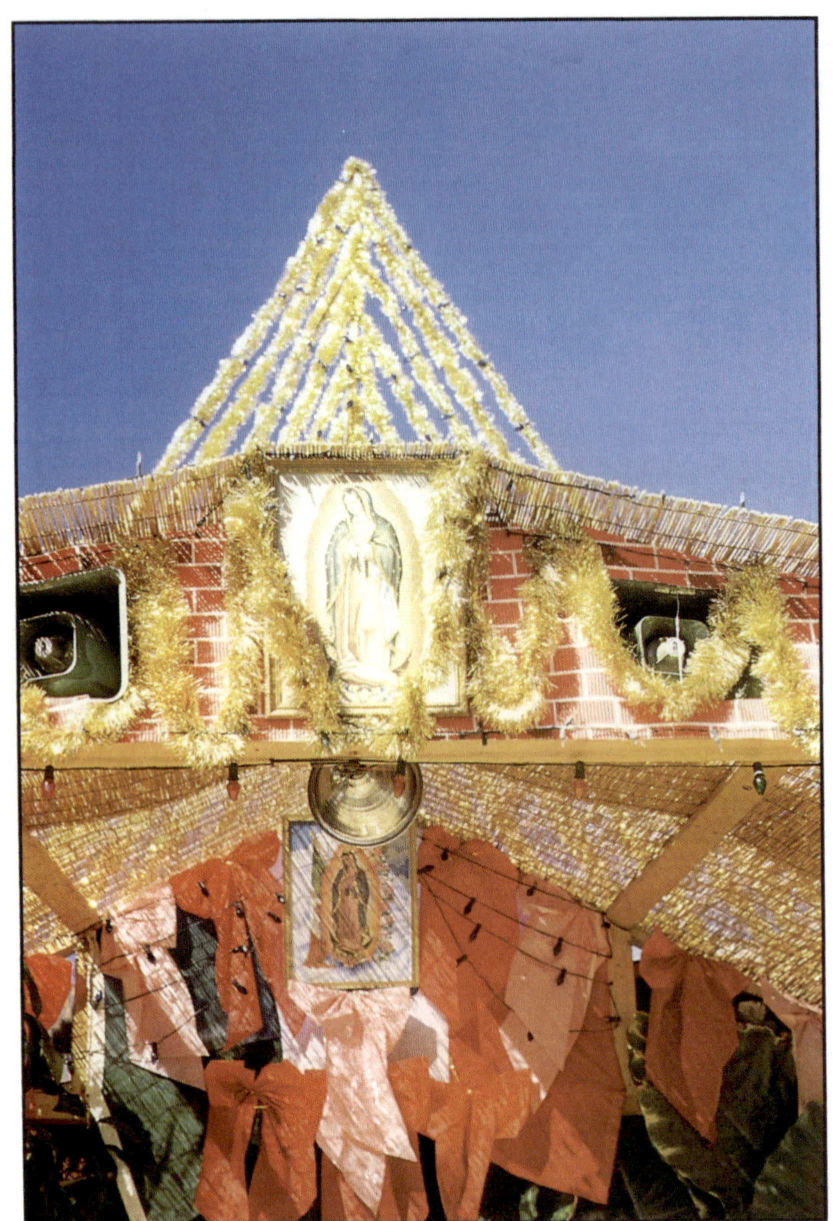

PLATE 25
Two chromolithographs of the Virgin of Guadalupe hang from the interior and exterior of the *ramada* (Christmas 1989).

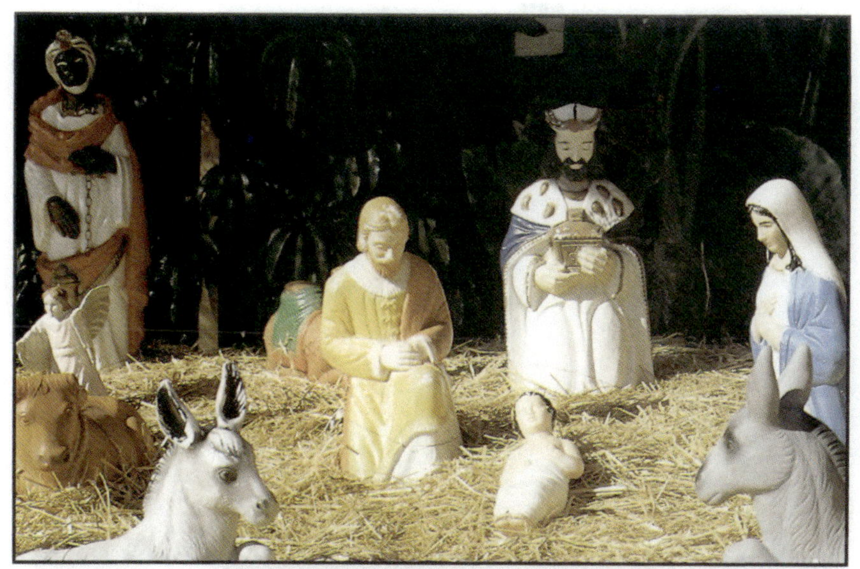

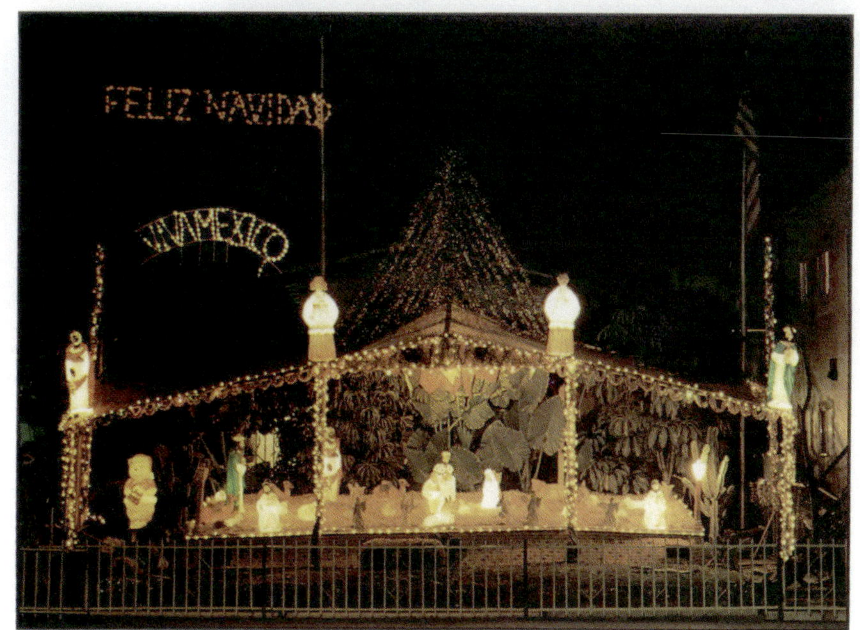

P L A T E 2 6
The Holy Birth takes place in the center of the scene (Christmas 1989).

P L A T E 2 7
The Christmas display at night (1989).

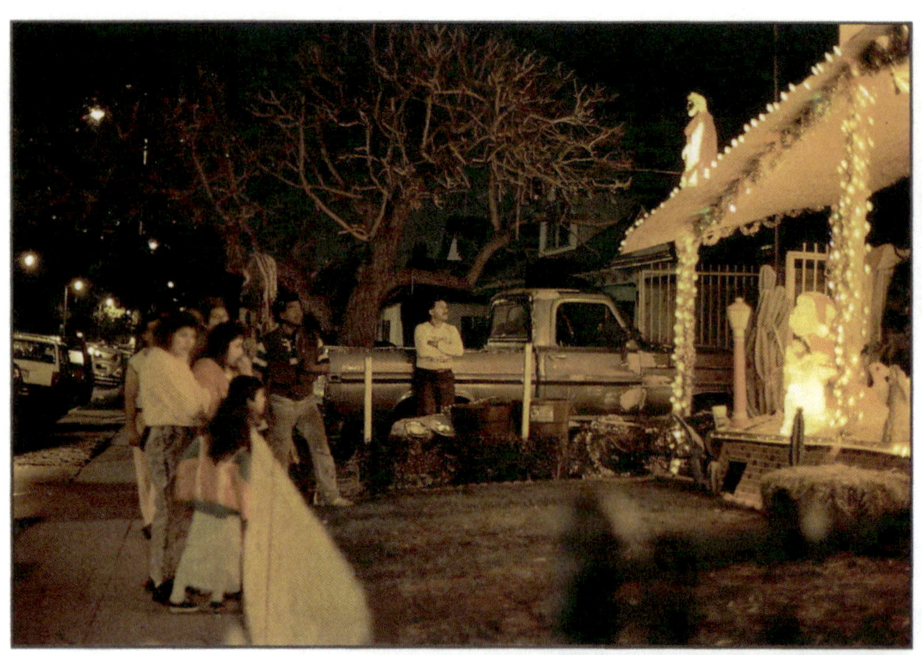

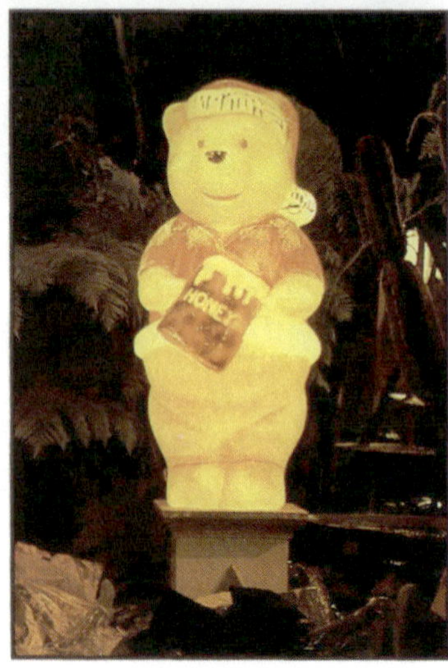

PLATE 28
Passersby admire Florencio's work-in-progress (Christmas 1989).

PLATE 29
The electric Pooh bear stands to the side of the Holy Birth (Christmas 1989).

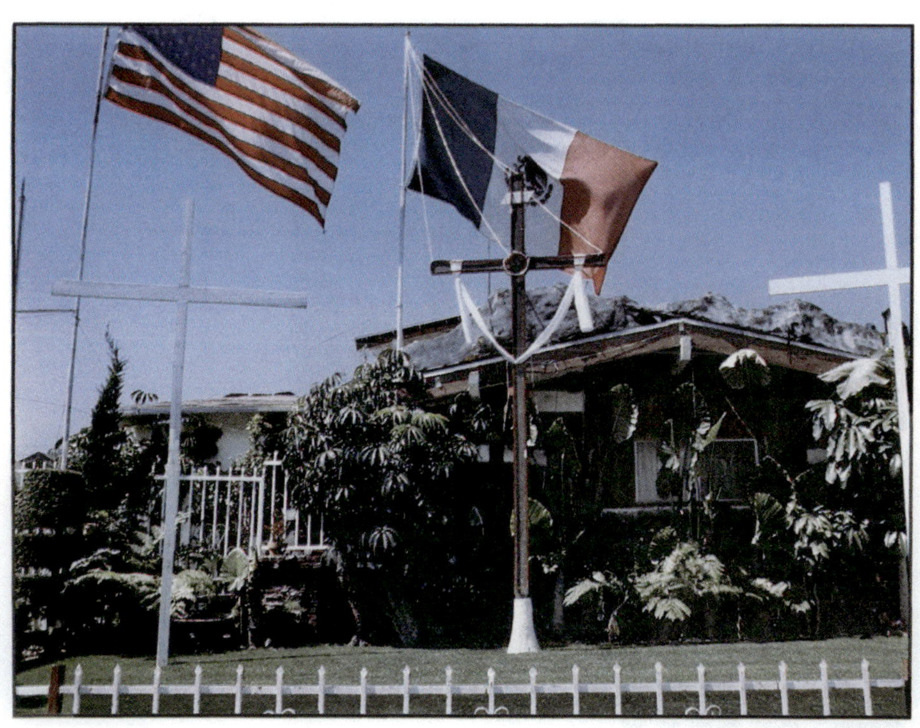

PLATE 30
The Easter display. At night the viewer sees the central cross bordered in red lights as well as an illuminated ring to represent Jesus's crown of thorns. An additional three strands of lights run from Christ's cross to the flagpole (between 1987 and 1989).

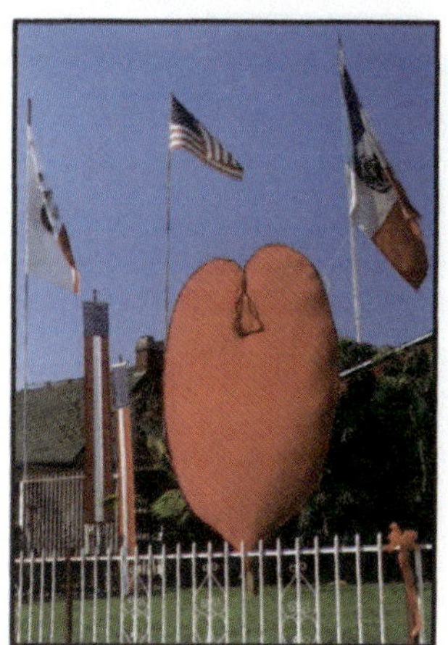

PLATE 31
Valentine's Day exhibit with the official colors of California, United States and Mexico (1990).

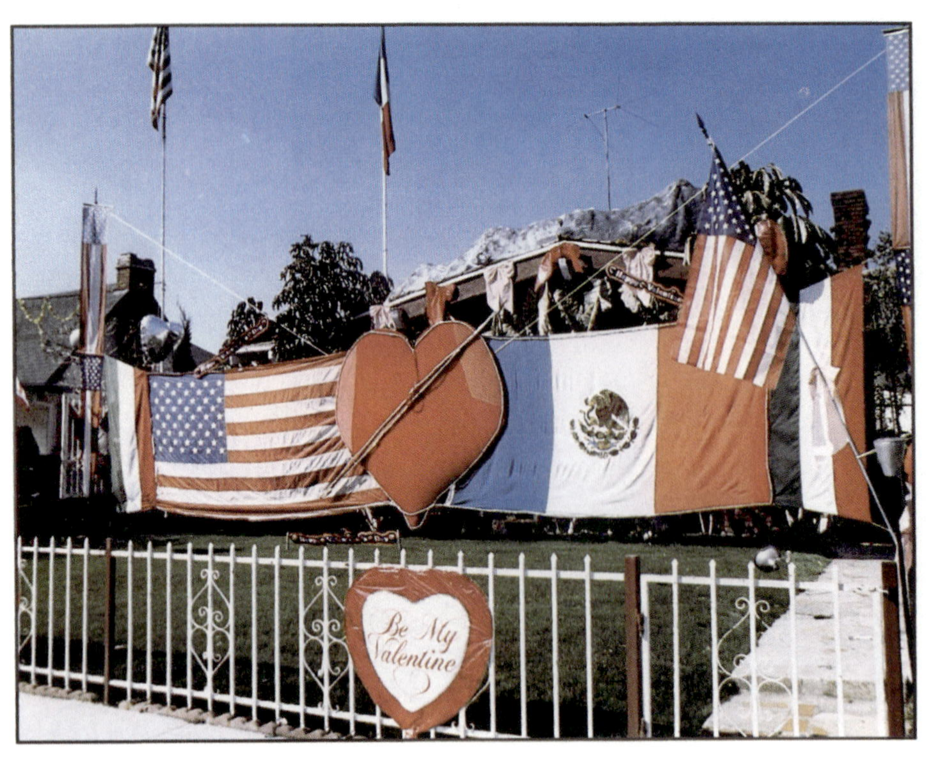

PLATE 32
Valentine's Day exhibit in 1991. This elaborated version includes a newly constructed arrow-pierced heart, rounder and wider than the original. Other significant additions are the huge American and Mexican flags that flank the heart. Besides declaring his love to those he held dear, perhaps Florencio meant to express his love for both of his countries.

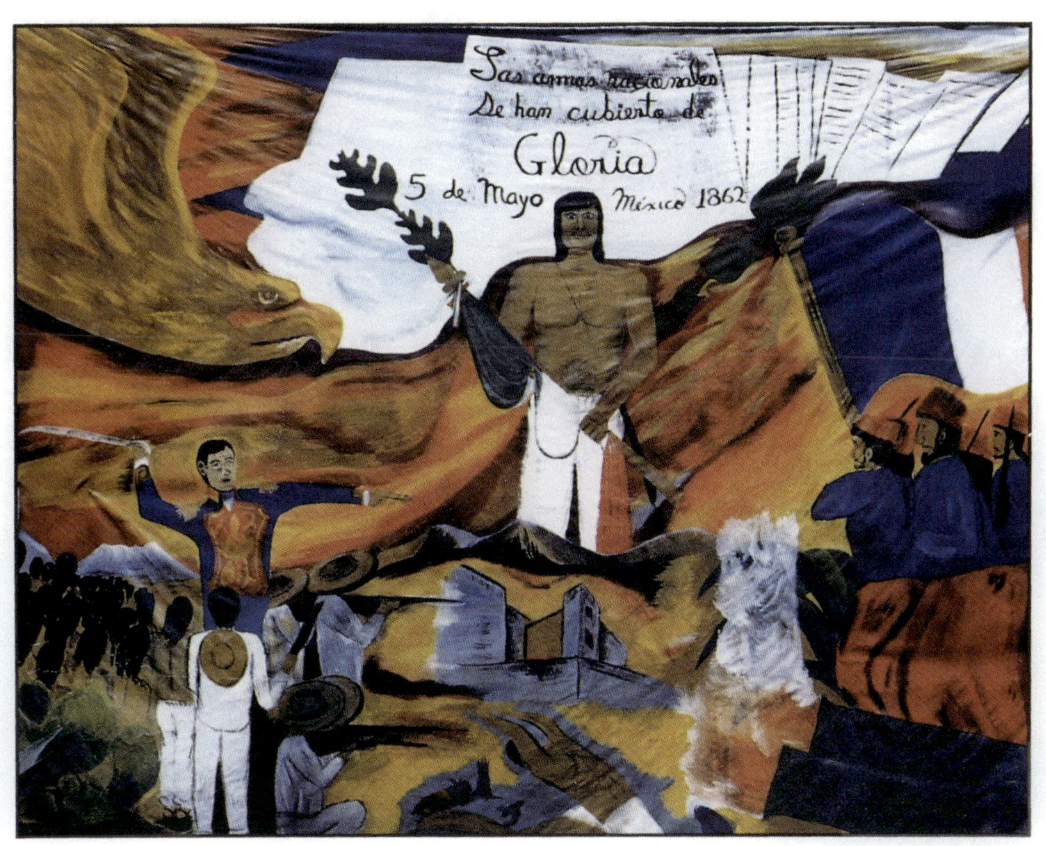

PLATE 33
Mural commemorating *Cinco de Mayo* (1990).

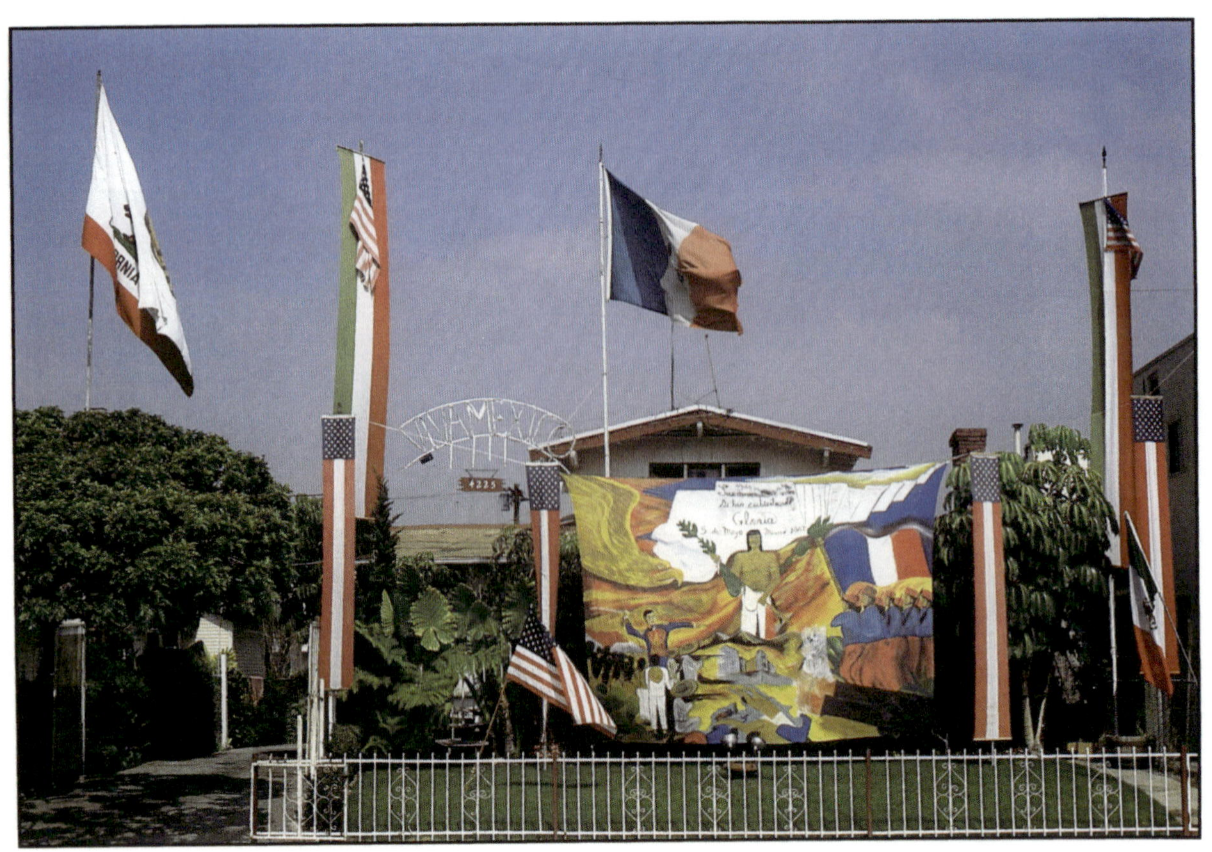

PLATE 34
Cinco de Mayo display (1990).

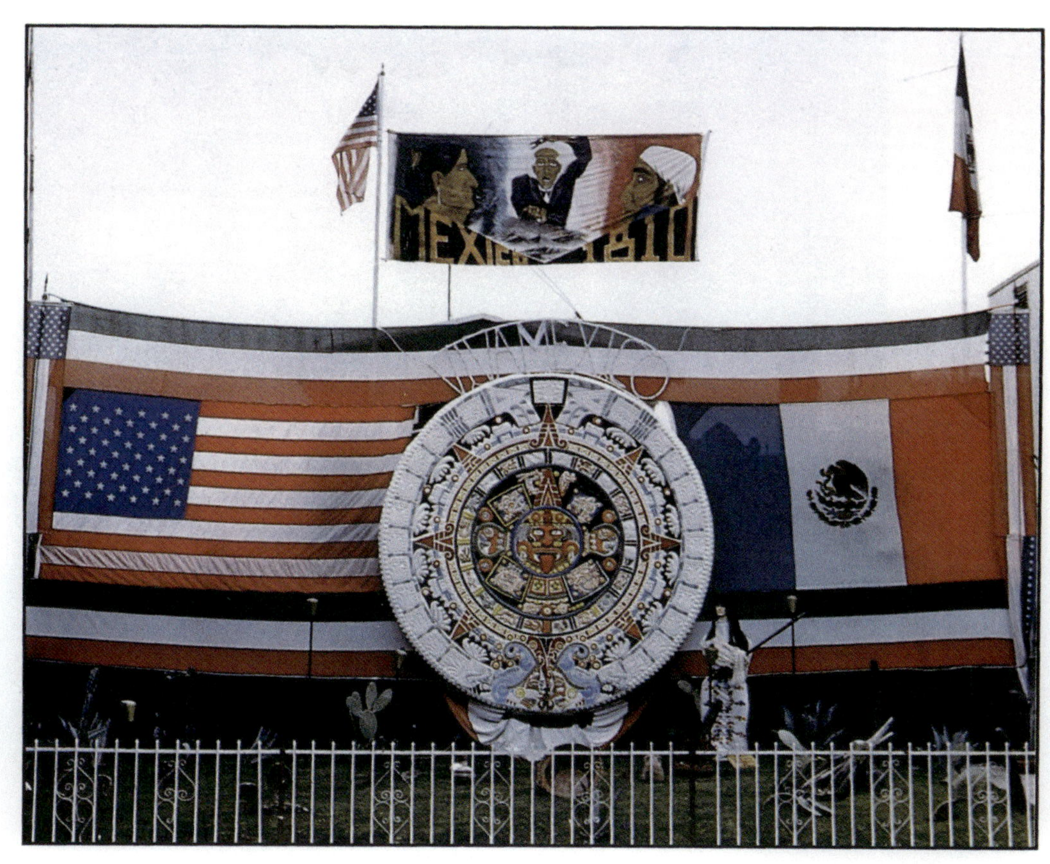

PLATE 35
Original Mexican Independence Day display (September 16, 1987 or 1988).

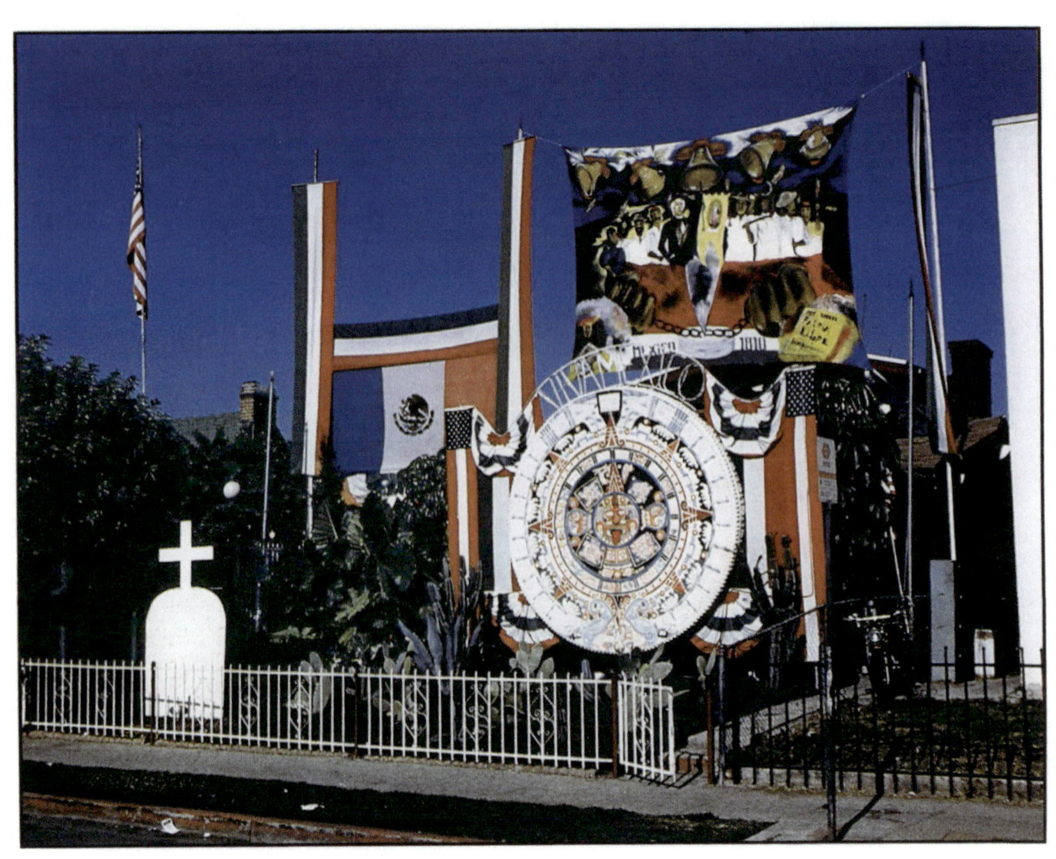

PLATE 36
Mexican Independence Day display (1991). This exhibit is a dramatic departure from the earlier installation.

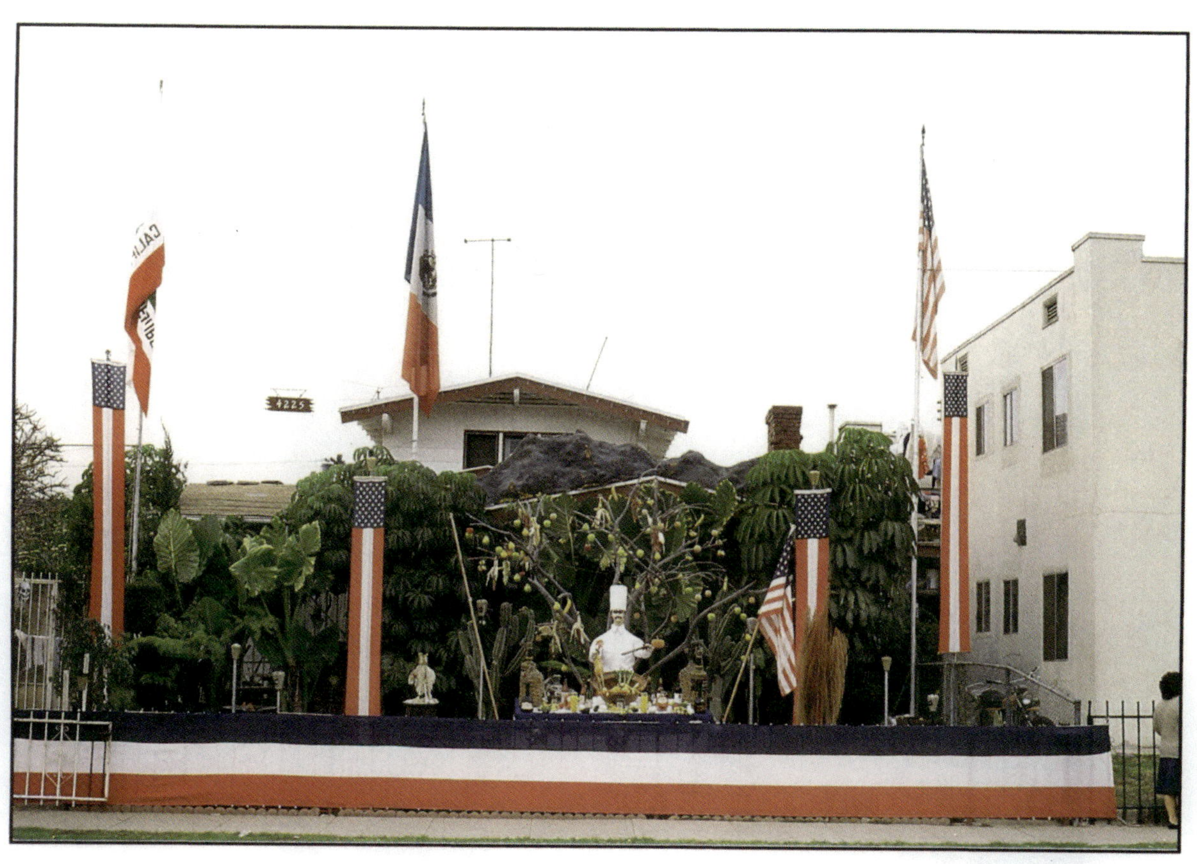

PLATE 37
Thanksgiving display (1989).

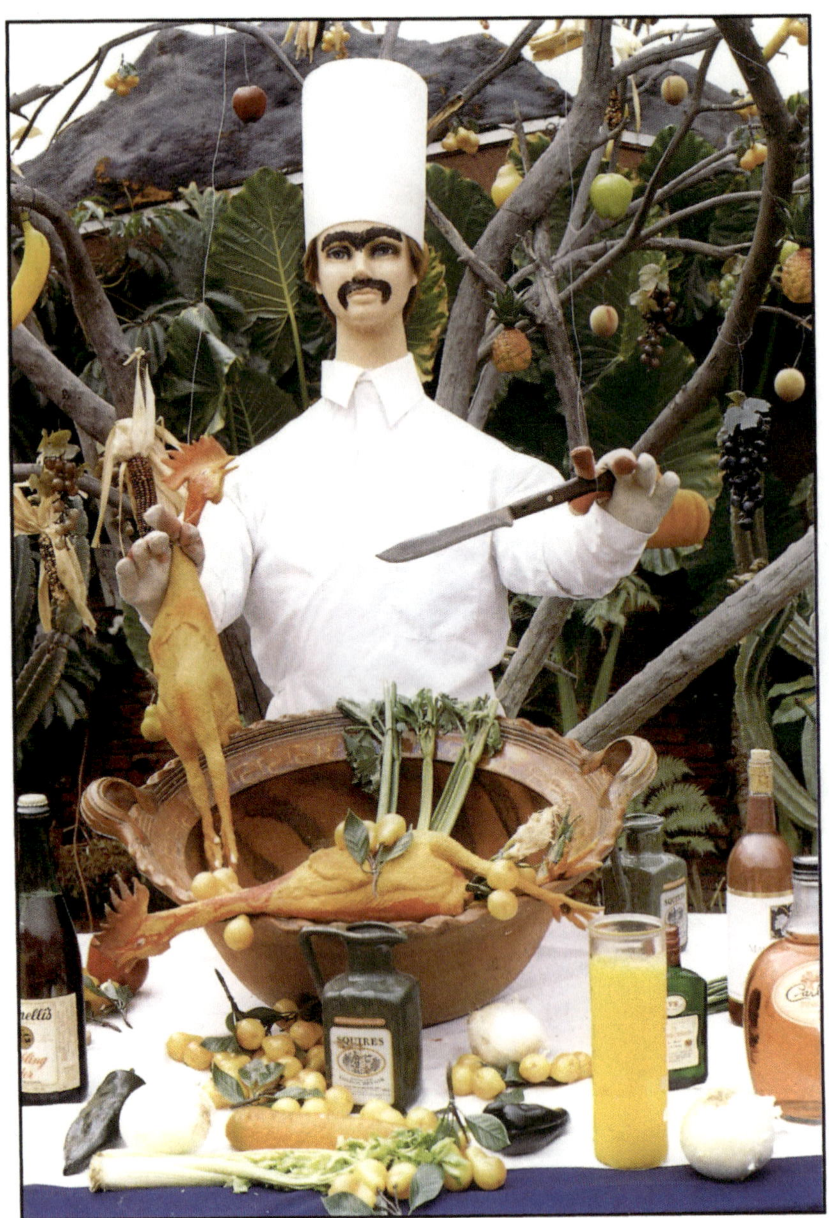

PLATE 38
Central figure of Thanksgiving display (1989).

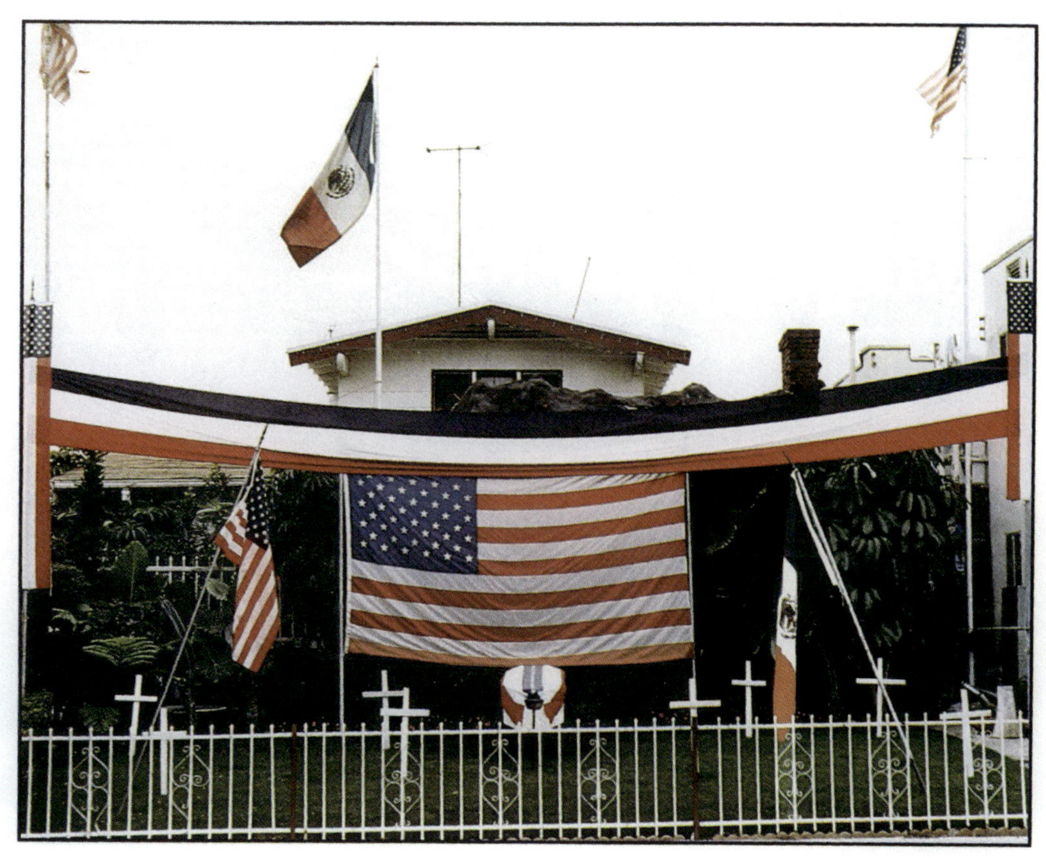

PLATE 39
Memorial Day display (between 1987 and 1989).

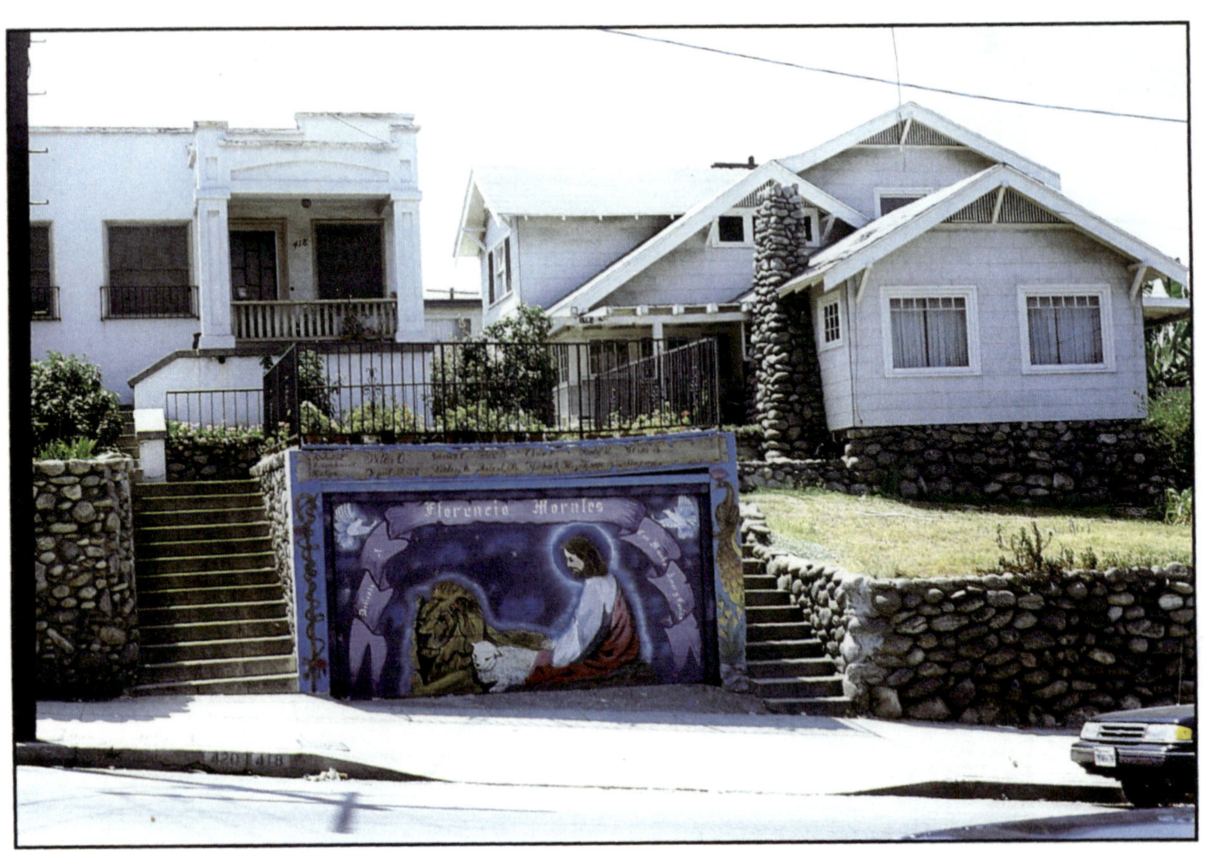

PLATE 40
Mural honoring Florencio Morales on Avenue 43 garage door created by Peter Quezada and neighborhood youth in April 1992. The artists' names appear on painted scroll above.

CPSIA information can be obtained at www.ICGtesting.com
Printed in the USA
BVIW12n0248131015
421102BV00006B/4

* 9 7 8 1 6 1 7 0 3 3 3 2 2 *